'Illegal' Traveller

*Global Ethics Series*

Series Editor: **Christien van den Anker**, Reader, Department of Politics, University of the West of England, UK

Global Ethics as a field builds on longer traditions of ethical reflection about (global) society and discusses ethical approaches to global issues. These include but are not limited to issues highlighted by the process of globalization (in the widest sense) and increasing multiculturalism. They also engage with migration, the environment, poverty and inequality, peace and conflict, human rights, global citizenship, social movements, and global governance. Despite fluid boundaries between fields, Global Ethics can be clearly marked out by its multidisciplinary approach, its interest in a strong link between theory, policy and practice and its inclusion of a range of work from strictly normative to more empirical.

Books in the series provide a specific normative approach, taxonomy, or an ethical position on a specific issue in Global Ethics through empirical work. They explicitly engage with Global Ethics as a field and position themselves in regard to existing debates even when outlining more local approaches or issues. The *Global Ethics Series* has been designed to reach beyond a liberal cosmopolitan agenda and engage with contextualism as well as structural analyses of injustice in current global politics and its disciplining discourses.

*Titles include*:

Carlos R. Cordourier-Real
TRANSNATIONAL SOCIAL JUSTICE

Anna Grear
REDIRECTING HUMAN RIGHTS
Facing the Challenge of Corporate Legal Humanity

Shahram Khosravi
'ILLEGAL' TRAVELLER
An Auto-Ethnography of Borders

Ivan Manokha *(editor)*
THE POLITICAL ECONOMY OF HUMAN RIGHTS ENFORCEMENT

Darrel Moellendorf
GLOBAL INEQUALITY MATTERS

**Global Ethics Series**
**Series Standing Order ISBN 978–0–230–01958–4**

You can receive future titles in this series as they are published by placing a standing order. Please contact your bookseller or, in case of difficulty, write to us at the address below with your name and address, the title of the series and the ISBN quoted above.

Customer Services Department, Macmillan Distribution Ltd, Houndmills, Basingstoke, Hampshire RG21 6XS, England

# 'Illegal' Traveller

## An Auto-Ethnography of Borders

*Shahram Khosravi*
*Associate Professor, Department of Social Anthropology,*
*Stockholm University, Sweden*

First published 2010 by
PALGRAVE MACMILLAN

Palgrave Macmillan in the UK is an imprint of Macmillan Publishers Limited, registered in England, company number 785998, of Houndmills, Basingstoke, Hampshire RG21 6XS.

Palgrave Macmillan in the US is a division of St Martin's Press LLC, 175 Fifth Avenue, New York, NY 10010.

Palgrave Macmillan is the global academic imprint of the above companies and has companies and representatives throughout the world.

Palgrave® and Macmillan® are registered trademarks in the United States, the United Kingdom, Europe and other countries.

ISBN: 978-0-230-23079-8 hardback

This book is printed on paper suitable for recycling and made from fully managed and sustained forest sources. Logging, pulping and manufacturing processes are expected to conform to the environmental regulations of the country of origin.

A catalogue record for this book is available from the British Library.

Library of Congress Cataloging-in-Publication Data

Khosravi, Shahram.
    "Illegal" traveller : an auto-ethnography of borders / Shahram Khosravi.
        p. cm.—(Global ethics series)
        ISBN 978-0-230-23079-8 (alk. paper)
        1. Emigration and immigration – Social aspects. 2. Boundaries – Social aspects. 3. Illegal aliens. 4. Khosravi, Shahram – Travel. 5. Iranians – Foreign countries – Biography. I. Title.
JV6225.K46 2010
304.8—dc22                                              2010007408

*To my defeated ancestors:*
*Walter Benjamin and Edward Said*

*When I return,*
*It will be with another man's clothes, another man's name.*
*My coming will be unexpected.*
*If you look at me unbelieving, and say, You are not he,*
*I will show you signs and you will believe me.*
*I will tell you about the lemon tree in your garden.*
*The corner window that lets in the moonlight*
*And then sings of the body, signs of love.*
*And as we climb trembling to our old room,*
*between one embrace and the next*
*Between lovers' calls, I will tell you about the journey, all the*
*    night long*
*And in all the nights to come,*
*Between one embrace and the next*
*Between lovers' calls, the whole human story.*
*The story that never ends.*

Theo Angelopoulos, *Ulysses' Gaze* (1995)
Free translation of Homer's *Ulysses*

# Contents

# Acknowledgements

Portions of this book appeared in an article in *Social Anthropology* 2007 (3). These portions are reproduced here with the permission of the European Association of Social Anthropologists.

I am deeply indebted to all those who generously shared their experiences and stories with me. Stateless individuals, undocumented migrants, failed asylum seekers, human smugglers, border people, whose words became material for this book. I am grateful to Helena Wulff, Kirin Narayan, Ulf Hannerz and Ilká Thiessen for their comments on early drafts; to Johan Lindquist and Paul Stoller for intellectual inspirations; to the Centre for Refugee Studies at York University, Toronto, where I wrote a first draft of this book in the summer of 2008; to Mahmood Arai for our long and inspiring conversations over countless cups of coffee; to Christien van den Anker who believed in this book and encouraged me to write it – her critical and insightful suggestions and comments have made this book better; to the Swedish Council for Working Life and Social Research for financial support; to Roxane, Maryam and Kian; to my father Nader; and, most of all, to my mother Parvaneh whose hospitality has no limit.

# Preface

## 1987

One cold night in late February, in a barren land surrounded by huge rugged mountains, I stood on a gravel road, like any other road in this rural area. Midnight passed; the whole landscape was wrapped in silence. The road separated Iran from Afghanistan. It *was* the border. Shrouded in a deadly stillness was the road; one of the most sanguinary borders in the world laid in wait for its next prey. It was a moonless night. 'Good! The darkness shelters us', said my smuggler. Indeed, it is not fair for him to be called a *smuggler*, as it was he who rescued me from certain death in a dreadful war. The gravel road separated two states, defining two sorts of human beings. It was not a road but a wall – according to law – invisible to the eyes.

'If I take a step', I thought, 'I will be somewhere else. When my foot touches the ground on the other side of the road, I will not be the same person. If I take this step, I will be an "illegal" person and the world will never be the same again'. That night I took that step and my odyssey of 'illegality' began.

## 2004

On 25 May, Fatemeh-Kian G.S., a 50-year-old Iranian transsexual, committed suicide in a detention centre north of Stockholm. She had fled Iran because of her sexual orientation and sought asylum in Sweden in November 2001. She had been arrested once by the moral police in Iran and been sentenced to 50 lashes for homosexuality. Her application for asylum was declined by the Swedish Migration Board in the last weeks of 2002 and again by a higher court in February 2004. She believed that she would be severely punished if she were sent back to Iran. Despite her lack of travel documents, the police attempted to take her forcibly to the Iranian embassy in late March 2004, but she resisted and refused to cooperate. She was placed in the detention centre in north Stockholm. A friend testified that the staff at the centre were annoyed by her lack of cooperation. She was isolated and her pleas for medical attention were ignored. Suffering from psychological stress and insomnia, her requests for medical treatment were met with disbelief and indifference. Abandoned and depressed, she attempted suicide in early May, but was saved by other detainees. She was hospitalized overnight and returned to the detention centre the next day, accused of faking suicide. Thereafter her psychological condition deteriorated.

The activists who met her in detention say that Fatemeh-Kian suffered constantly from dizziness and stress. She also had physical injuries. Her friend who saw Fatemeh-Kian's body in the mortuary photographed her feet, which were badly injured. Fatemeh-Kian asked for help just four days before her death, saying that she was sick and could not sleep. She asked to see a doctor but her request was ignored. On 25 May, the staff of the centre found Fatemeh-Kian dead in her room. Alone and disbelieved, she had committed suicide with anti-depressant pills. It later emerged that there was no documentation of her first suicide attempt and that staff at the centre had not been informed of her psychological condition.

Fatemeh-Kian G.S. who, according to case workers and friends was an atheist, was buried in the Muslim section of a cemetery near the detention centre, and a simple metal grave marker in the shape of a *cross* was put on her grave. When I visited her grave in January 2007, there was still no gravestone to say who was buried there. The municipal council argued that local tax revenues should not be used for a gravestone for Fatemeh-Kian.

The agony of her life and death, her bodily, sexual, and geographical displacement, her journey for hope and loss of hope in the Swedish detention centre, and finally her displacement even after death – alienhood completed – opened my eyes to the world I live in.

# Introduction

This book is about borders and border transgressors. The paradigmatic image of the world today is undoubtedly one of bodies, squeezed between pallets inside a truck. The picture is taken by an X-ray camera on a border between nation-states. It exposes those that are invisible, the people without papers on the wrong side of the border. The X-ray image shows the naked, white bodies on a black background – a silhouette of human beings. Metaphorically, human bodies are also stripped: of their political rights. The image depicts a depoliticized body, in Giorgio Agamben's words, the *homo sacer* (1998), personifying 'the naked life', which differs from the politicized form of life explicitly represented in the notion of citizenship. The X-ray image testifies to a hegemonic topography of borders.

Ours is a time of the triumph of borders, an epoch of border fetishism. Borders determine how the world looks. The map represents the world as a mosaic of unities, of nations, with clear outlines and distinct in different colours. Borders are constructed to designate difference. Today's political map resembles, in Ernest Gellner's words, Modigliani's painting style: 'neat flat surfaces are clearly separated from each other, it is generally plain where one begins and another ends, and there is little if any ambiguity or overlap' (Gellner 1990:139–140). There is no intermission between borders. Borders appear unbreakable as if they have always been there. Natural barriers, such as rivers, mountains and deserts, are used to designate borders, and thereby to naturalize them. In this way, borders are presented as primordial, timeless, as part of nature.

Borders symbolize the sovereignty of states. A nation-state can be imagined (Anderson 1983) only through its borders. The nation-state system is based on the functional nexus between a determinate localization (territory) and a determinate order (the state), a nexus mediated by automatic regulations for inscription of life, individual or national (Agamben 2000:42). In the nation-state system, *zoé*, naked biological life, is immediately transformed into *bios*, political life or citizenship. The link between life/birth and the nation becomes obviously naturalized in language. The terms 'native' and 'nation' have the same Latin root as does the word for birth, *nascere*.

The borders of nation-states have come to constitute a natural order in many dimensions of human life (Malkki 1995a:5). Borders are no longer the simple edges of a state. 'Borders shape our perception of the world ... border thinking is a major component of our consciousness of the world' (Rumford 2006:166). Borders are the essential reference of communal sense, of identity. They are not only external realities but also 'colour bars' situated everywhere and nowhere (Balibar 2002:78).

The *national* order of things usually passes as the normal or *natural* order of things. It is self-evident that 'real' nations are fixed in space and marked by their borders (Malkki 1992:26). Malkki argues that naturalizing the border regime leads to a vision of border crossing as pathological (1992:34). Displacement – or, in the botanical jargon of the national order of things, uprootedness – is believed to result in an 'unnatural' mode of being. Border transgressors break the link between 'nativity' and nationality and bring the nation-state system into crisis.

According to this view, violation of the border regime is a violation of ethical and aesthetic norms. If in the nation-state system unidentified asylum seekers and undocumented immigrants represent such 'a disquieting element, it is above all because by breaking up the identity between man and citizen, between nativity and nationality, [they] throw into crisis the original fiction of sovereignty' (Agamben 1995). It is not surprising that they are seen as a political and symbolic threat to national sovereignty or purity. In *Purity and Danger* (1966), Mary Douglas explored how distinguishing purity from impurity is a mechanism for preserving social structure and for determining what is morally acceptable. Undocumented migrants and unauthorized border crossers are polluted and polluting because of their very unclassifiability (Malkki 1995a; 1995b). As 'transitional beings [they] are particularly polluting, since they are neither one thing nor another; or maybe both; or neither here nor there...and are at the very least "betwixt and between" all the recognized fixed points in the space-time of cultural classification' (Turner 1967:97).

Through politico–juridical discourse and regulation, this system creates a politicized human being (a citizen of a nation-state) but also a by-product, a politically unidentifiable 'leftover', a 'no-longer-human being' (Schütz 2000:121). Sent back and forth between sovereign states, humiliated, and represented as polluted and polluting bodies, stateless asylum seekers and irregular migrants are excluded and become the detritus of humanity, leading wasted lives (Rajaram and Grundy-Warr 2004). The modern nation-state has claimed the right to preside over the distinction between useful (legitimate) and wasted (illegitimate) lives (Bauman 2004:33).

These wasted lives are the *homo sacer* of the present. Agamben (1998) uses the term *homo sacer* from Roman law to describe an existence and condition that he describes as 'naked life'. The *homo sacer* is one who has been stripped of membership in society and thereby of his or her rights. According to Roman law, *homines sacri* could be killed without it being considered murder. The *homo sacer* is reduced from a complete political being to a simple biological or natural body, stripped of all rights. Agamben believes that the system of nation-states differentiates between naked (depoliticized) life (*zoé*) and a political form of life (*bios*). The *homo sacer* is a completely depoliticized body different from the politicized forms of life, embodied in the citizen (Rajaram and Grundy-Warr 2004). In their capacity as *homines sacri*, irregular immigrants are left vulnerable not only to state violence (through regulations, political arrangements, laws, priorities, and police) but also to the violence of ordinary citizens, without being able to protect or defend themselves (Rajaram and Grundy-Warr 2004:57).

'Illegal' border crossing challenges the sacramental aspect of the border rituals and symbols. Moreover, it is seen as a criminal act deserving punishment. The border system is governed by criminalization: as Simon (2007) puts it, 'governing·through crime' makes crime and punishment the institutional context whereby a criminal population (for example, the poor, 'illegal' immigrants, asylum seekers, and 'terrorists') is constructed and excluded (see also Rose 1999:259). The justification for governing by criminalization is to protect citizens from the threats of *anti-citizens* (see Inda 2006). Criminals, poor people, homeless people, undocumented immigrants, and unidentified asylum seekers are all seen as threats to the wellbeing of the social body. Immigration penality 'constitutes and enforces borders, polices non-citizens, identifies those deemed dangerous, diseased, deceitful, or destitute, and refuses them entry or casts them out' (Pratt 2005:1). Targeting undesirable non-citizens, governing by criminalization, is done by enforcing harsher external and internal border controls, confinement, and forced deportation. The border is performed by the state on the travelling bodies (Wilson and Weber 2008).

For some people – all kinds of migrants and people who live along borders – crossing borders is an inescapable feature of life; it is a mode of being in the world (Willen 2007). Based on a racially discriminating way of thinking, borders regulate movements of people. While a small category of people enjoy unrestricted mobility rights, most people are caught within borders. The regulation of mobility operates through social sorting that involves sexual, gender, racial and class inequalities. The social sorting of travellers starts long before they reach the border (Wilson and Weber 2008). Travellers from 'suspect' nations are subjected to a high degree of control via a stringent visa process.

Borders, however, are also spaces of defiance and resistance. 'Illegal' border crossing and borders are defined in terms of each other: the existence of borders is the very basis of this form of travelling (Donnan and Wilson 1999:101). Migration and borders are also defined in relation to each other. Where there is a border, there is also border crossing, legal as well as illegal.

## The form

This book is written in an auto-ethnographical style, with personal experiences interjected into ethnographic writing. As a form of self-narrative, auto-ethnography 'places the self within a social context' (Reed-Danahay 1997:9). It 'displays multiple layers of consciousness, connecting the personal to the cultural' (Ellis and Bochner 2000:739).

Unlike depersonalized narrative, auto-ethnography asks its 'readers to feel the truth of their stories and to become coparticipants, engaging the storyline morally, emotionally, aesthetically, and intellectually' (Ellis and Bochner 2000:745).

This book is not an autobiography, but an ethnography of borders. Based on my own journey and my informants' border narratives, I will tell of the nature of borders, border politics, and the rituals and performances of border crossing. Auto-ethnography lets migrants contextualize their accounts of the experience of migrant illegality. It helps us explore abstract concepts of policy and law and translate them into cultural terms grounded in everyday life. Furthermore, focusing on the individual also draws attention to the *implementation* of policy and law, which produces different insights from focusing narrowly on legislation and formal documents per se (cf. van der Leun 2003). Border stories reveal the interaction between agency and structure in the migratory experiences. They offer a human portrait of 'illegal' travellers.

This book is the outgrowth of my own 'embodied experience of borders', of ethnographic fieldwork among undocumented migrants between 2004 and 2008, and of teaching courses on irregular migration and the anthropology of borders. It also emerges from my activities outside academia: freelance journalism, helping arrange events such as film festivals about border crossing, and volunteer work for non-governmental organizations (NGOs) helping failed asylum seekers and undocumented migrants in Sweden.

In my years as an anthropologist, I have been astonished at how my informants' experiences overlapped, confirmed, completed, and recalled my own experiences of borders. One interesting aspect of the auto-ethnographic text is that the distinction between ethnographer and 'others' is unclear. Similarities between informants' subjective experiences and my own blur the distinction between anthropologist and informants. This challenges imposed identities and boundaries and offers forms of meaning alternative to the dominant discourse (Pratt 1992). Auto-ethnography links the world of the author with the world of others. It bridges the gap between the anthropologist's reality and the reality of others.

This book has also emerged from 'thinking poetically', that is, 'keeping alive a sense of what it means to live in the world one struggles to understand' (Jackson 2007:xii). Through poetic thinking, one does not focus either on one's own subjectivity or on the objectivity of the world, but on what emerges from the space between (Stoller 2009).

Studies of migrant illegality are often written by people who have never experienced it; my aim has been to offer an alternative, partly first-hand, account of unauthorized border crossing that attempts to read the world through 'illegal' eyes. I tell the story of those whose history has been crushed underfoot. Like Benjamin in his work on *The Arcade Project*, I am a 'ragpicker'. I pick up the refuse of history, gather all that is disregarded. Following Benjamin, I believe that 'waste materials are to enter into significant connections and fragments are used to gain a new perspective on history' (Benjamin 2007:252–253). I collect stories of the 'illegals': stateless people, failed asylum seekers, undocumented and unregistered people, those who are hidden and clandestine.

Like the *testimonios* in Latin America, a tradition that confers authority on subaltern voices (Warren 1997), this auto-ethnography gains its narrative power from the concept of witnessing. The significance of the voice of the witness is that the witness has been there, has seen what happened. Witnesses have themselves lived the disaster, and might themselves be victims. They can retell the story and unfold the event with first-hand authority. This does not mean that witnesses, just because they are insiders, possess the only authentic approach. The witness's narrative is only one of many, albeit one less heard.

In *Theses on the Concept of History* (1999 [1940]), Benjamin writes about a Paul Klee painting entitled 'Angelus Novus'. In the ninth thesis, he describes an angel flying over the ruins of history. His face is towards the past; he is looking back, resisting forgetfulness. He would like to pause and piece together what has been ruined. But a strong storm – a metaphor for progress – from Paradise is blowing, driving him irresistibly into the future, to which his back is turned. In this book I intend just this: to delay, to look back and tell the story of the refuse of history, the story of the defeated – to two of whom (victims of the borders) this book is dedicated. However, rather than simply being a memoir of the past, the mixed voices here convey a warning for the future.

This book is an essay, recalling the meaning of the French *essayer*, to try. My hope is that the reader will experience this book like a journey on a ring road, returning at the journey's end to the starting point, but with unanswered questions, inexplicable problems, unsatisfied curiosity and unfulfilled expectations. The reader will nevertheless have encountered many people and things along the way. I have *tried*, following Walter Benjamin's example, to *show* things, not tell them.

# 1
## Accustomed Soil

There is hope, but not for us.

Kafka

One winter day in 1986, I received a letter from the army. I had finished high school one year before and neglected to register myself for the compulsory two-year military service. A horrible war had been going on between Iran and Iraq since 1980. Hundreds of thousands of young men, many in their teenage years, had been killed, many more lost body parts or were gravely injured by chemical weapons. A few years earlier, in my second and third years of high school, several of my classmates (16 and 17 years old) were martyred along with our theology teacher – who always came to class in military uniform. They had gone to the front as *basiji*, members of the volunteer militia, who provided the teenage 'human wave' in the war against Iraq. So many students from my school were killed that its name – Adab – was changed to Martyrs of Adab (Shohaday-e Adab).

Half a million Iranian youths are estimated to have lost their lives in the war (Amani 1992). The state used all available means to promote a 'martyrdom-seeking attitude' (*rouhi-ye shahadat talabi*) among the nation's youth. Martyrdom was regarded as analogous to 'sweet syrup', drunk by those ready for self-sacrifice. The official notice of a son's death on the battlefield, delivered to his family, regularly began: 'Congratulations and condolences' (*tabrik va tasliat*). Media propaganda incessantly showed warriors who expressed their wish to become martyrs, awaiting their martyrdom with joy and triumph. Returnees from the frontlines even complained that they

8

had been 'disqualified' from being martyrs (*liyaqat-e shahadat nad-ashtan*). The symbolism of martyrdom was all-prevalent in Iranian society: there were exhibitions and workshops on martyrdom, and other activities were arranged, such as live theatre. Schools even sent their students to visit puppet performances on the theme of martyrdom.

Martyrdom came to dominate urban spaces and official culture. A huge organization emerged to handle martyrdom-related cultural activities, commissioning large murals of martyrs around the city, publishing 'war literature' and collecting slang expressions and war memoirs for publication in the series 'Culture of the Front' (*Farhang-e Jebhe*). In Tehran alone, 1400 streets had their names changed to the names of martyrs (Chelkowski and Dabashi 1999:121). Furthermore, the state supported a new cinema genre called 'Cinema of the Holy Defence'. Up to 10 per cent of the readings in textbooks from the second through fifth grades (for children between 8 and 12 years old) concern death and martyrdom (Nafisi 1992:168). Interviews with the families of martyrs were featured in media programming every day. The six Iranian TV channels, all state-owned, played a crucial role in reproducing the hegemonic grief-stricken ethos.

Martyrdom was not depicted as merely death, but as a desirable fate. One day, on a break between two lessons, we gathered around a classmate who had just returned from the war front. He had spent the whole summer and almost the whole fall at the front. He, whose name I forget, was 16 or 17 years old, thin and taller than average. He talked enthusiastically about his war experiences. We all listened in silence. The silence was even more intensified while he was recounting how he killed his first Iraqi soldier. His coldness in recounting the homicide was disturbing. The war had made killing and being killed ordinary happenings in our everyday lives. They had become 'natural'. The young boy from the war zone told of his first homicide as if he were telling of his first sexual experience.

For us in school, going to *jebhe* (the war front) was not just a religious task, or an act of patriotism, but also a matter of masculinity, of showing off our manhood. Our classmate was a *man* now, his masculinity proved. The dialectic relationship between the experience of killing – usually animals – and the production of masculinity is found in many societies. For young Bakhtiari men, the entrance to adulthood was made through hunting. When I took my first life at the age of 15, by killing a rock partridge, the rite of passage was launched. I was not religious, though, nor a patriot, and my masculinity was far from worth dying or killing for, so I chose to go into hiding after finishing high school.

I started a clandestine life that resembled the life of undocumented migrants. I was a clandestine person in my own country, a fact that cast a shadow on every aspect of my life. I could not work, study, travel, buy or sell properties, or even get married. I was in exile in my hometown. Military police controlled the roads to and from the cities. They also regularly patrolled the streets to catch 'conscientious objectors' like me. I spent much of the year on my father's place in the country in the Bakhtiari mountains. The letter from the army was the 'last' call. Tired of being a fugitive without any future, I had decided to give up and join the army. In the afternoon of the day the letter arrived, I went to the kitchen to tell my mother of my decision. Behind a mound of vegetables, she was preparing dinner.

Our home was always filled with expected and unexpected guests. I can never remember a day when we – that is, my parents, older brother, two sisters (one older and one younger), and myself – were alone. Hospitality, *khone dar baz bodan*– providing a house with open doors – was a holy tradition in our tribal culture. The door of our house was literally always open. My parents were from Bakhtiari 'middle' khan (tribal leader) families. My father was the 'big man' in the extended family, a respected man with a large farm and a great many people around him. As a real Bakhtiari man, he was an excellent hunter, owning several rifles and horses. The story of his hunting a bear when he was barely 25 years old is well-known to everybody in the region. In their youth, my parents had established a footing in Isfahan (Iran's second largest city), and our life oscillated between urban and tribal life. I grew up, in some ways, in a bicultural milieu. As an ethnic minority, we found Isfahan unfamiliar and somehow unfriendly.

We lived in a Jewish quarter, among another minority group. I have two strong, clear memories of my 'un-belonging' in urban Iran. One is from my first year at school at the age of seven. I did not speak Farsi fluently and my accent made my classmates laugh. I still have a clear mental image of the class of laughing kids. The other memory is from my early teenage years, in middle school. One day, when I was heading to drink from a water fountain in the corner of our schoolyard, a classmate 'warned' me not to drink from the fountain because a 'Jewish' classmate had just drunk from it. Although the latter did not offend me personally it pushed me anyway into an alienhood.

Furthermore Bakhtiaris were systematically harassed for wearing their traditional clothes in Isfahan. Women wearing long colourful skirts with many layers, long scarves which can contain ornaments and decorations sewn in from faux coins to hand-sewn designs and men in their black wide, skirt-like trousers and round black hats were called names and laughed at. These incidents have had a strong impact on my sense of 'outsiderness' in urban Iran. Exile, many years later, reopened the old sores, as experiences of one exile recall another. Exclusion in Sweden recalled these memories, reminding me that the homeland is not always home.

Although we were somehow incorporated (economically but not socially or culturally) into society, Isfahan was never *home* for us. We lived in Isfahan but had a Bakhtiari lifestyle. Isfahani people were always strangers to us, and we to them. They were city people, we were tribal and we experienced Iran differently. The 'stability' and emergence of the nation-state under the Pahlavis (1925–1979) meant suffering and loss to us. My maternal grandfathers were imprisoned, and my mother's uncles and cousin as well. Many of them were executed by Reza Shah in the 1930s. Later on, the modernization policy of the 1950s and 1960s (for example, the White Revolution) meant confiscation of my paternal properties (for more details on the oppression of the Bakhtiari see Tapper 1983 and Garthwaite 2009).

The Islamic Revolution of 1979 changed our lives drastically and intensified our 'outsiderness'. In the eyes of the theocracy, we tribal people were of 'low culture' and therefore were not as 'authentically' Muslim as urbanites were. Hundreds of missionaries were sent to the villages to teach us what 'authentic' Islam was, how to dress, pray, behave, etc. Though the Islamic Republic brought more social justice to rural areas and to nomadic people, it brought political adversity to my family. My father, accused of being involved in an anti-revolutionary movement, was imprisoned in 1980. One night, when he was alone in our house in Bakhtiari area, they took him. It was around midnight when a large number of Revolutionary Guards broke in, as if they had expected to find a militia group inside our house. For a long time, no one knew where my father was or why he was detained. The authorities did not answer our questions or simply denied that they had arrested him. Meanwhile, we read in the newspaper that he, alongside two other Bakhtiari men, were to be executed. He, however, was released after six months and then exiled from the Bakhtiari for several years. Some of his property was confiscated and he was banned from travelling abroad, a ban that has persisted ever since. Everyone associated with him was marked as 'anti-revolutionary'. This meant that making a career in education or another profession became an unattainable dream for us.

I was never a 'proper' citizen of the Islamic Republic, anyway. In high school, I never participated in pro-state activities and ceremonies. I was repeatedly warned and disciplined by the Islamic Association (*Anjoman-e Eslami*) of the high school for my 'un-Islamic behaviours'. Like many other young Iranians, I took pride in defiance (see Khosravi 2008). Although my modest defiance resulted merely in trivial and short-term victories, it gave me a feeling of being alive. My noncompliance was sometimes too costly. At age 18, I was arrested, together with two friends, for purchasing illicit alcoholic beverages on the black market. We were sentenced to flogging, 30 lashes each.

That winter day in 1986, in the kitchen, my mother listened silently to my argument about joining the army. After a while, she advised me to wait until my father had returned from the country. I said I could not live clandestinely any more and had to join the army before the deadline passed. Without looking at me, while her fingers picked, cleaned and cut the vegetables, she said flatly, 'No, I do not let you'. My mother knew well that my avoiding army service meant long-term separation from me. Seeking a safe haven outside the country was the only option. That afternoon, in the kitchen behind a mound of vegetables, she, *my mother*, saved me from certain death in a long and bloody war. She *saved* me. Not by 'heroic' words or acts, but modestly, while chopping tomatoes and chives.

We had no tradition of migration in our family. Tehran was the farthest place my parents had ever visited. Attachment to Khanemirza, our place in Bakhtiari area, was stronger than any desire to see other places in Iran, let alone outside the country. My older brother was forced to go to London to study before the Revolution. He suffered six months before my father let him return. Our whole existence was constructed around our old and beautiful building (built by my great-grandfather) in the middle of a grove of hazelnut trees, and surrounded by huge mountains, Sivak, Kousor (Red Mountain) and Kousozo (Green Mountain). For my father, *zamin* – earth, land – meant more than just property. It was his honour (*ezat*), his background and history, his place in life. While his cousins and relatives sold their lands to invest in the city, he planted hazelnut trees or planned a vineyard. My attachment was not just to the place, but much more strongly to the people among whom I grew up, the people of the village and those who worked for us. I spent the whole fall, winter and spring in Isfahan, longing unbearably for Khanemirza. The summers were like a dream: I spent days with farmers on their farms, followed herders on their excursions with sheep and goats, or hiked hours to visit nomads in the nearby mountains. In the afternoons, driven by the hot sun, with other children we took refuge in the calm gardens and talked and played endlessly. Sometimes we went bathing in a brook that passed our village. My childhood was safe and full of tenderness, generosity and caring. To go and leave all this would be unforgivable.

There is a tendency in migration studies to rank migrants along a continuum of choice, ranging from free (voluntary migration) at one end to not-free (forced migration) at the other (see Turton 2003). In migration studies, forced migrants are usually represented as without agency. Lacking any kind of choice or option, they are victims of socio-political structures that force them to move. Richmond (1994), for example, distinguishes between 'reactive' (forced) and 'proactive' (voluntary) migration. While he cites slavery as an example of the former, the latter is associated with tourism. Turton (2003) correctly argues that, in most reactive/forced migratory situations, people have more choice and elements of agency than migration theory allows. Even in cases of the most enforced type of migration, there is still room for choice. This choice is formed, of course, by age, class and gender. I was forced to choose between participating in war or leaving the country, but I still had a choice. Many others remained. Their choices were determined by lack of capital (like my friend Mansoor), attachment to the land (like another friend, Siamak), belief in religion, or by other factors. The circumstances surrounding migration are multi-faceted. One crucial factor in the migration process is the existence of a 'culture of migration'.

A culture of migration comprises 'those ideas, practices and cultural artefacts that reinforce the celebration of migration and migrants' (Ali 2007:39). A 'culture of migration' exists when migration is pervasive, has historical presence and the decision to migrate is part of everyday experience (Cohen 2004:5; Hahn and Klute 2007). Not only among Bakhtiaris but among all Iranians, international migration was not commonplace until the 1980s. Mass migration from Iran started only after the 1979 Islamic Revolution. Until then, Iranian migration was limited to guest students or a small number of guest workers in Kuwait. Naturally, there was no culture of migration, so migration was not a learned social behaviour and we had not learned to desire to migrate. A 'culture of migration' emerges when migration becomes so deeply rooted that the prospect of movement becomes normative. For instance, for young Mexicans, migration to the USA has become a normal part of the course of their lives (Kandel and Massey 2002;).

Among Bakhtiaris, migration was not accepted by most people, and I have long been blamed by my relatives for having abandoned my parents. Migration is a product and has its own process. The decision to migrate, the initial phase of the migratory process, entails huge psychological struggles for the migrant and the people around him or her. It is a critical decision that forever changes the lives of many people involved, whether directly or peripherally. 'Illegal' migration can mean a lifelong separation from family, friends, home. It is a journey of adversity, peril, deterioration, physical pain and tears. It is a journey of indefinite route, length, cost and destination. You do not know what to expect and no one expects you.

The next phase of the migration process is preparing for the journey. Providing capital for the journey is crucial. Financial resources determine the degree of danger. Massive capital could make the 'illegal' journey safe, easy and short, by air through the international airport of Tehran. Limited financial resources could mean crossing the border on foot in remote and dangerous fringes of the country.

My parents would finance my journey, but we needed information, networks, infrastructure. In the absence of a 'culture of migration', there was no 'migration industry' to facilitate the process of migration. All we had was rumours. None of us knew exactly what to do until a friend of my uncle, whose son had fled to Pakistan, helped us contact a 'middleman'. The middleman who located clients for a human smuggler ushered in the passage to the third phase, the journey itself.

# 2
# Border Guards and Border People

In September 1986, a 'middleman' took me to Iranshahr, a small city in the province of Baluchistan near the border with Pakistan. He was the link to a local human smuggler. We arrived in the afternoon and checked into a small, cheap hotel, the owner of which was the smuggler. What I did not know was that the smuggler was collaborating with the police. He, as we later found out, gave the 'small fry' to the police to be allowed to take the 'big ones'. In the middle of the night I was awakened by the sound of a Nissan Patrol, a four-wheel-drive SUV used by the Revolutionary Guards. The fear was embodied. Like many other young people in Iran, I was vigilant for signs of peril, such as the sound of a Nissan Patrol. My clandestine life was shaped by various 'somatic modes of attention' (Willen 2007:17). I looked out the window, without turning on the light. A Nissan Patrol was there, parked in front of the main entrance. The next minute, the Revolutionary Guards were pounding on the door.

In the first week in custody, no one answered my questions nor was I asked any questions. I do not know what happened to the middleman, as I never saw him again. Was he also involved with the border police? After seven days, long middle-of-the-night interrogations began. During the interrogations, my eyes were covered with a large piece of cloth that also covered my nose. It smelled sour, of dried sweat. Every time it was put over my face, I wondered whose sweat had dried on it. The smell testified to a suffering body. Endless questions, covered eyes, threats and unexpected punches made me sweat, too. My sweat was absorbed in the piece of cloth and blended with others', to tell the next body of our fear and pain. I denied that

I was leaving the country, though the questions indicated that the smuggler or the middleman had confessed everything. However, from previous experience, I knew that one should deny accusations, no matter how obviously true. I insisted that I was just travelling around. The questioning ended when the interrogators were convinced that I was not a political activist. After ten days, when I was transferred to a prison, I was first allowed to make a call. It was early morning and my mother picked up the phone, hoping to hear my voice from the other side of the border.

In custody and later in prison, everybody I met had been arrested in connection with the border. For more than a month, I was in cells with small and large drug smugglers, undocumented Afghan migrants, a dozen young men like myself who had tried to flee the country, and local native Baluchi tribesmen who for generations had crossed the border freely, but were now being punished for violating the nation-state system. Large drug smugglers paid and stayed no more than one or two nights, but Afghans without documents, who had already been robbed by bandits or border guards, stayed longer. It was a small prison, and border transgressors were numerous. Crowded into dirty, overcrowded cells, some nights we took turns sleeping – half sat up while the other half lay down. Sometimes I was put in small cells that I shared with others. One of them was known in prison as 'Mohammad the Short Leg', a Pakistani citizen who was serving a long sentence for drug smuggling. After several years in prison, he got leave twice a year. He visited his home village on the other side of the border and came back again to prison, where he at least had food.

As mentioned before, locals constituted the majority of the 100 people in prison; only 12 of us were non-Baluchi Iranians. All interrogators and guards were non-Baluchi Iranians moved there from other parts of the country. Baluchi inmates came from poor backgrounds and made decorative *chilims* (hookahs), selling them outside to support their families. Despite their poverty, I witnessed acts of noble generosity by Baluchi inmates. On visiting days, they gave us, the non-local inmates who had no visitors, food and fruit their families had brought them. Even in prison, where they were socially, economically and politically underprivileged compared with non-Baluchi Iranians, they regarded us as guests to their region. The poverty was and still is extreme among those who live along the border in this region. At the same time, this border is one of the most profit-able in the world for smugglers, traffickers and corrupt border guards.

Much of the 909-kilometer-long border with Pakistan and the 936-kilometer border with Afghanstan is extremely porous, particu-larly the southern Afghan border with Iran. The Afghanstan–Iranian border is the fifth most trafficked migration corridor in the world (World Bank 2008). The harsh terrain of the region makes it easy to avoid immigration checkpoints. Consequently, drug smuggling and human trafficking across this border are huge in scale (see IOM 2008). Young girls are trafficked from Iran to Pakistan and from Afghanstan to Iran for sexual exploitation. Boys from northern Afghanstan (mainly from the Farsi/Dari-speaking Hazara ethnic group) are trafficked for forced labour in Iran, while minors from southern Afghanstan (mainly Pashtuns) are trafficked to Pakistan for forced prostitution and begging. Similarly, young boys from Bangladesh and Pakistan are trafficked to Iran en route to the Gulf States, where they are forced to work as camel jockeys, beggars and labourers. Afghan refugees and undocumented migrants seek a future in Iran, either as their country of destination or in transit to Europe. Thousands of Iranian refugees were smuggled to Pakistan and Afghanstan in the 1980s and 1990s.

This border is as undefined as the destiny of Afghanstan. The lives of many Afghans is affected, regulated and circumscribed by this border. An almost 30-year-long occupation and civil war since 1979 has resulted in the displacement of millions of Afghan people. Since the early 1980s, Iran has been a main destination country for between two and three million Afghan refugees and migrants. As of 2005, the number of registered Afghan refugees in Iran had declined to one million (World Refugee Survey 2007) while the total number of Afghans in Iran was estimated at up to two million at any time (IOM 2008). Unlike Afghan expatriates in Pakistan, who have been located mainly in refugee camps near the border (such as Jalozai in north-eastern Pakistan with 80,000 refugees), Afghan refugees in Iran have settled in large cities from the beginning. Afghan refugees have made up a considerable part of the labour force in the construction and agriculture sectors. Taking the whole population of Afghanistan to be approximately 30 million, almost 6.6 per cent of Afghan people live and work in Iran. This means that one of every 15 Afghans is or has been to Iran at one time or another. It is hard to imagine a single family in all Afghanstan that is not affected by the Afghan–Iranian migratory system. Many families in Afghanstan are reliant on remittances sent by young workers from Iran, which are estimated at around USD 500 million annually, equivalent to 6 per cent of Afghanstan's GDP (cf. Kronenfeld 2008).

Furthermore, much of the world's opium is produced in Afghanstan (Afghanistan Opium Survey 2007) and finds its way to Europe through Iran. Up to 90 per cent of the heroin consumed in Europe crosses this border (Gouverneur 2002). A combination of human smuggling and trafficking and drug smuggling has made this border a lucrative place, causing insecurity and considerable violence for border people. Bandits occasionally cross the border to kidnap people and to plunder and raid border villages. In response, 50,000 Iranian soldiers and policemen are posted along the border from Turkmenistan in the north to the Indian Ocean in the south. There are several hundred checkpoints, dozens of walls blocking mountain passes and nearly 500 kilometres of barbed wire, none of which has been able to bring security to the border. A war continues between the armed forces and the smugglers. The heavily armed gangs dominate the border region at night. According to Iranian officials, more than 3000 Iranian soldiers have been killed on duty in this region over the past two decades (Gouverneur 2002).

In contrast to the common perception that 'borders are a boon for traffickers and a nightmare for law-enforcement agencies' (Rumford 2006:164), borders are beneficial even for some border guards. Undocumented border crossers are robbed by border guards before being taken into custody. Even legal border crossers are not safe. In prison, I met Pakistani pilgrims who were robbed by guards when they were legally crossing the border; when they protested, they were arrested. Bribery is also a common source of income among border guards. In prison, there were also several police officers accused of taking bribes from border crossers. I heard frequently that the best place to do military service was along the Iran–Pakistan border. One young man who did his military service on this border told me that in his 18 months of service in a border post he managed to save enough to buy a small apartment in his hometown of Isfahan. Not surprisingly, the border people usually view the various border officials, not the smugglers, as the true criminals (cf. McMurray

2001:123). Reported abuses, such as extortion, assault and rape, of migrants by Mexican and Guatemalan officials are almost equivalent to those perpetrated by bandits (Hagan 2008:73).

The current border regime indirectly fosters human smuggling, and a dialectical interplay between borders and human smuggling is at work. When an undocumented migrant is deported by the authorities, he or she comes back again the same day or a few days later. Each deportee is a new client for human smugglers. This is the case for Indonesians in Malaysia, Mexicans in the USA, Zimbabwean migrants in South Africa, and Afghan ones in Iran. Human smugglers target recent deportees at their arrival, who often have little or no money left, and offer assistance for immediate re-entry under the condition of working to repay the smuggling debt at high interest. Like the ironically named 'safe houses' for newcomer Chinese in New York, young Afghans are held hostage in eastern Iran by human traffickers who extort money from their families.

Insecurity in this region also arises from the discrimination against and persecution of border people. Baluchistan is divided by the Iran–Pakistan border, and the rights of Baluchis as Iranian citizens fade away in front of the authorities because of their religion, ethnic background and darker skin. Furthermore, this border region is also home to a large number of first- and second-generation undocumented Afghans, who live in a 'space of non-existence' (Coutin 2003), outside officially recognized rights, rules and norms (Monsutti 2007; Sadr 1386/2007).

I was released on bail after one month. It was a brief and gloomy farewell ceremony with my cellmates. For more than a month we had talked incessantly about our families, wishes and sorrows, past and future. I had many *chilims* (hookahs) to hand over to the families of my new Baluchi friends. I had the phone numbers of many families, so I could call and assure them of their son's, husband's or brother's wellbeing. Majid, one of my cellmates and a petty drug dealer, was released some time after me. I wanted to invite him to Isfahan, but my parents strictly forbade me to bring home a 'drug dealer'. Majid told me later that Mohmood Baluch, as we called him, had been executed. He was just a few years older than I. He had killed one person in a tribal conflict. During my time in prison, the connotations of labels such as 'dealer', 'smuggler' and 'thief' changed for me. When injustice and inequality become as pervasive as they are along this border, ethical assessments lose their weight. I spent the first night outside prison shivering with fever, distracted from all my fears for that night. A few months later, I was acquitted in court. I pledged never to go back to the border region again, but to enlist myself for military service.

## Human smugglers and the sacrifice of border transgressors

Five months later, I tried to leave again. This time I did not turn to a smuggler. An Afghan friend from prison put me in contact with Homayoun, a young Afghan man who worked as a construction worker in Tehran. Only a few years older than I, he had lived and worked clandestinely in Iran since he was 15. As an unaccompanied minor, he had come to Iran so that his younger siblings could go to school, thanks to the remittances he sent home. His parents were still living in Kabul under Soviet occupation. One January day in 1987, he called me and said that he was planning to visit Kabul to marry 'the most beautiful girl in Kabul'. He asked whether I wanted to come along. Homayoun requested USD 500 to take me to Quetta, the largest city in northeastern Pakistan. It was less than half the price my first smuggler had demanded. I had never considered Homayoun as a *smuggler*. Himself an undocumented migrant, Homayoun facilitated my escape from undesired martyrdom in a long and bloody war. Human smuggling is recurrently misrepresented by the media and politicians as an entirely 'mafia'-controlled criminality, but this is not the case.

The criminalization of migration has become central to the policy of governing through crime (Simon 2007). It creates criminals to be able to punish them. Redefining a social issue as crime, and categorizing an affected group as criminals, is a political strategy to legitimate further intervention into matters not previously regarded as criminal (Dauvergne 2008).

Furthermore, it is also usual not to differentiate between human smuggling and trafficking in people. Human smuggling is multifaceted and is a complex market of highly differentiated services (see Bilger, Hofmann and Jandl 2006; Liempt 2007). Moreover, various actors are involved who conduct sequential operations on different levels (see İçduygu and Toktas 2002). Human smugglers are not a homogenous group. Alongside the criminal ones, there are local people, such as nomads living in border regions for whom border crossing has become crucial to their economic and social life. They might facilitate an 'illegal' border crossing for a low price.

From my time in the border prison, I had learned enough to avoid falling into the trap again. I knew that one's risk of arrest increases every minute in a border city. I asked Homayoun if we could leave Iran the same day I arrived in the border city. To justify to the police my presence in a border city, I had obtained a forged student card that said I was studying at a university in Zahedan, at the centre of Baluchistan province. The date of the next attempt was the last week of February 1987.

Separation from family is an expected consequence of migration, and irregular migration puts enormous distance between family members extended across time and space. Migration without documents is a one-way road, and there is no turning back once you step onto it. My flight to Zahedan from Isfahan started early in the morning. At the time of parting from my parents and siblings, I did not know when I would see them again, if ever. In that early morning when the city's rush had yet to start, the sun was still behind the buildings and neighbouring houses were in an enviable calmness, I left my *home*. I knew that the tranquil street soon would be filled with children on their way to school and their parents to their jobs. The old lady in the house across from us would go, large bag in hand, on her daily tour to the fruit and vegetable bazaar, and vendors' voices would disturb those still in bed. Dr Ruben, our Jewish neighbour, my grandfather's afternoon tea companion and our family doctor, would, in his dark blue suit, black thick-framed glasses and white shirt, jump on his big Chinese bicycle and head to his clinic. That morning was, for others, just like any other morning. For me, the sorrow was excruciating. After two decades, memory of that morning still evokes enormous pain. I kissed my 12-year-old sister in her sleep. I preferred not to see her tears, which would have torn me apart. My father stayed in his room. The unbearable grief of separation paralysed him, making him unable to perform the farewell ceremony. My sister told me later that he did not come out of the room for two days. He did not eat, and did not talk. Through the window, they saw him sitting on the chair, bent forward and staring downward. I heard later from my sister that he blamed himself. He, the 'big man', the bear hunter, a man from whom many, even strangers, sought protection, could not protect his own son. My brother, who would take me to the airport, was waiting in the car. In my mother's embrace, the outside world, war, migration, borders, future and past all ceased to exist. I breathed her smell, the smell of my childhood, probably the first smell I experienced in my life, until she took a step backward and muttered something like 'Go!' My older sister poured water behind me when I crossed the threshold, an Iranian ritual expressing hope that the traveller shall come back soon. I did not turn back, did not look back. I could not. But in the car, I could no longer keep my eyes away from my mother. She stood at the door, not crying so as not to discourage me. But she was shaking. I knew that a storm was wracking every cell in her heart, as it was doing in mine. When my brother put the car in gear, I could not breathe any more and my tears poured out. Since then they have not ceased to run.

To cope with the unbearable burden of my departure, my mother sought consolation in faith. She made innumerable *nazr*s (vows to God) for my safety on my long and risky journey. Among Mexican migrants on their way into the USA, the *promesa* has a similar function (see Hagan 2008). At takeoff, the sense of uprooting was tangible, and I felt I was being pulled from my accustomed soil. I arrived in Zahedan around noon. A taxi took me to a marketplace in a suburb, where I was to meet Homayoun. The market was crammed with Afghan migrants in their traditional clothes and, in my jeans and T-shirt with a sack in my hand, I signalled 'I will be smuggled'. Passing police patrols made me anxious. Afghan vendors noticed this and let me hide behind their carts. I could not imagine the consequences of being arrested again. Homayoun showed up after half an hour or so; he took me to a house, brought me some food and said that I should get some rest. We waited until nightfall, as darkness would help us through checkpoints on the road.

We left Zahedan in the evening on a pickup, driving north for some hours towards the city of Zabol. At the checkpoint, I was squeezed under the dashboard and other people's legs. We took a side road to the east after the checkpoint. At some point the car stopped, and we were told to jump down and run towards the silhouette of huge mountains that separated Iran from Afghanstan. At the foot of the mountains, I changed from my jeans and T-shirt into Afghan national dress, which Homayoun had bought in the bazaar that day. We began to climb. It was a pitch-dark night and I tried to stay very close to Homayoun. Although I trusted him, I had heard stories of how smugglers just disappeared in the night and left their clients alone, which meant certain death. On reaching each summit, Homayoun pointed eastward and said that the border was behind the next peak. After several hours, we did reach the border – a gravelled road as open as any other road in countryside, yet closed by law. We hid ourselves behind bushes near the border, waiting in silence for half an hour or so, to check whether any border guards were around. It was cold and we were freezing, but we could not move until we were sure it was safe. Homayoun asked me to wait while he went to do a safety check. I did not want to be left alone but had no option. During that short time of maybe ten minutes, I was sure that he would not come back.

Like the nights I slept under the open sky in the Bakhtiari, the clear, dark sky offered an amazing spectacle of stars. I tried to find my position by those stars in case Homayoun did not show up, so I'd be able to go back. But he did; it was safe and we hurried towards the border. With a few steps, I crossed the border and so began my odyssey, outside all regulations and laws, without travel documents and across many national borders. There I was, on the other side of the border – without papers, on the same earth, just a few steps away, yet the soil was not the same. I, my body, identity and culture were 'out of place', out of their place. In conventional terms, I had become 'uprooted', condemned to wither. A woeful destiny for those who do not abide by the rules of border.

When I crossed the border, I was full of ambiguous feelings. I was overwhelmed by a sense of guilt about all those young men who did not want to or could not leave and were going to certain death at the war front. This sense of guilt was gradually transformed into a sense of shame, which gets stronger with the years of exile. I left behind my family, friends, neighbours and many others in danger. Isfahan, like other large cities, was attacked by missiles at least once a day. I left behind Mansoor, a friend from a poor family, who could not afford migration. He was furthermore the oldest son of the family and was supposed to take care of his elderly parents. He was sent to the war front when I was in Pakistan.

Armed with only an AK-47 in his hands, he was sent against Saddam Hussein's ultra-modern army backed by the USA and several European states. Mansoor and many others like him, without masks or other equipment, had no chance when Hussein launched his chemical warfare. More than 20 years later, Mansoor suffers from excruciating pain, as the poison has irremediably damaged his lungs. As I write these words in March 2009, he cannot work any more. He cannot even walk more than ten metres without resting. Not educated and not Farsi speaking, he got lost in the bureaucratic labyrinth and was not approved for government compensation. The shame of having left him and so many other young men behind is inevitable.

We kept going all night without rest. Once, Homayoun said that he was not sure whether we were headed in the right direction and, approaching dawn, we saw a border watchtower, which Homayoun said belonged to Pakistan. We began to run in the opposite direction. The guards, Homayoun said, would shoot to kill, not to warn or arrest. After 13 hours climbing and walking, we finally reached a camp in Nimroz province. It was a sort of self-organized internally displaced persons camp for those who had fled the Red Army. It was 1987 and Afghanstan was still occupied by the Soviet Union. The camp was not large and consisted of around a hundred tents. There was no running water nor any other basic facilities. I saw no trace of any international organizations – it was a forgotten camp on the most remote frontier of Afghanstan. A militia group, perhaps the Afghan Mujaheddin, which was supported by the Iranian government, with whom they had extensive military collaboration, controlled it, and there were numerous trucks mounted with heavy weapons. All the men carried arms. For a few dollars, an old man let us hide in his shelter. He gave us tea and bread, which he said was the only food in the camp.

We arrived in the camp on a Friday, the Muslim Sabbath. At noon, the militiamen searched the tents and forced people to attend Friday prayers. A young man with a Kalashnikov in his hands found me and asked who I was. Homayoun intervened and asked me to go outside. After a while, the Kalashnikov-carrying man left us alone. He had probably been paid by Homayoun to ignore my presence in the camp. After this incident, Homayoun decided to leave the camp as soon as possible – the Kalashnikov-man would certainly come back again. Homayoun said that he would follow me all the way to Karachi: my insistence that he give priority to his fiancée waiting for him in Kabul fell on deaf ears.

Homayoun was short and thin with a crooked smile always on his face. In Afghan dress he seemed even tinier. He was from the Hazara ethnic minority (Shiite, Dari speaking) who constitute 9 per cent of the total Afghan population. Since the beginnings of modern Afghanstan in the mid-eighteenth century, Hazara people have faced persecution at the hands of the majority Pashtuns (Sunni, 42 percent of the population) and have been forcibly displaced. I had never seen him in his national dress in Iran. He said later that to avoid racial harassment in Tehran, he did not wear Afghan dress. When I asked him about racism in Iran, he would answer, perhaps not to offend me, 'The sky has the same colour everywhere'. 'The sky has the same colour' to some people, no matter where they happen to be, exposed to a continuum of exclusion and discrimination. In one place an outcast, in another an outsider. As Franz Kafka once said, 'there is hope, but not for us' – unsurprisingly cynical words from a German-speaking Jew living in Prague. Kafka embodied the continuum of exclusion, experiencing the same colour of the sky everywhere, in his three identities: among the people of Prague, he was not only Jewish but also German speaking, and among German-speaking Jews he was Czech.

In the eyes of the law, Homayoun was a human smuggler, a law breaker and a criminal. But in fact, he saved my life in one of the most dangerous places on earth, under the rule of ruthless criminal gangs, corrupt border guards and the Afghan Mujaheddin. Hagan, working from Mexican and Central American migrants' testimony, stresses the role of coyotes in ensuring the safety of the migrants (2008:78). In the process of criminalizing migration, human smugglers become scapegoats. They are held responsible for all migrant deaths at borders. The authorities represent human smugglers as criminals. The vast majority of migrant deaths, usually by drowning, in the sea along Spanish–African borders happen in relation to interception activities by Spanish border guards (Carling 2007). Not everyone was as lucky as I was to have had a good 'guide' and 'facilitator'. Later in Karachi, I heard horrible stories of rape, homicide, kidnapping and blackmail of people on the borders by their smugglers.

Hagan correctly points out that not all border crossers face similar levels or types of danger. Political circumstances, geographical factors, the migrant's gender, the composition of the migrant's companions, the mode of crossing all determine the level of danger (2008:61).

## Dehumanization of border transgressors

An 'illegal' traveller is in a space of lawlessness, outside the protection of the law. This is the main feature of contemporary border politics. It *exposes* the border transgressors to death rather than directly using its power to kill (Agamben 1998; Mbembe 2003). The vulnerability of border transgressors is best demonstrated by their 'animalization'. The terminology in this field is full of names of animals designating human smugglers and their clients: *coyote* for the human smuggler and *pollos* (chickens) for Mexican border crossers (Donnan and Wilson 1999:135); *shetou* (snakehead) for Chinese human smugglers and *renshe* (human snakes) for smuggled Chinese (Chin 1999:187). Iranians usually use the terms *gosfand* (sheep) or *dar poste gosfand* (in the skin of sheep) to refer to 'illegal' border crossers. Dehumanized and represented in terms of chicken and sheep – two animals traditionally sacrificed in rituals – the border transgressors are sacrificial creatures for the border ritual.

The x-ray images taken of containers and trucks crossing borders depict the bodies of unauthorized border crossers squeezed between banana boxes or other cargos. Their bodies are reduced to merchandise, to commodities, fungible and disposable. One restaurant owner in central Stockholm answered my question on the difference between legal and undocumented migrants this way: 'An illegal migrant has a red "sale" sticker on him. Fifty per cent off'. What is left of these migrants is bodies whose only 'value' is assessed in terms of how much force they can engender. A telling example of the dehumanization of unauthorized border crossers can be seen in the Hollywood science fiction movie *Men in Black*. The movie, as it appears on promotional posters, is about 'protecting the earth from the scum of the universe'. The hero, an Immigration and Naturalization Service (INS) agent, chases space aliens, non-human creatures. The movie starts with a 'humorous mistake'. Instead of space aliens, a group of human aliens – undocumented Mexican border transgressors – are apprehended. Metaphorically, the unauthorized border crossers are equated with alien space organisms, the 'scum of the universe'. Human 'alien' is conflated with 'space alien'. The movie, however, goes further in dehumanizing border crossers, when it shows the body of one undocumented Mexican border crosser acting as host to a parasitic alien space creature, the 'scum of the universe' (Marciniak 2006; Hicks 2007).

In Colombia, to be *displazdo* or *desplazada* is to be placed between the human and non-human (Agier 2008:15). The use of vocabulary such as 'dog wagons' (for transporting apprehended unauthorized border crossers) and 'hunting' (for chasing unauthorized migrants) by the Minutemen along the Mexican-US border demonstrate the degree to which border crossers have become dehumanized (Michalowski 2007:69). If not non-human, border transgressors are seen as less human and thereby eligible for sacrifice. The borders that separate the rich from the poor world demand more sacrifice than do the borders separating poor countries from each other. 'The US–Mexican border is where the third world grates against the first and bleeds' (Anzaldúa 1987:12). Today, the borders between poor world and rich world are turned into an exhibit of death (Inda 2007:148). Not unexpectedly, the highest rate of sacrifice of border transgressors takes place on the Mexico–USA border and on the borders of Fortress Europe. While the former on average demands 500 sacrificial human beings per year, the latter on average demands more than 700 lives. On average more than three persons die daily along these borders. From January 1993 to May 2009 more than 13,250 refugees and migrants have died in attempting to entering Fortress Europe, a figure that includes only documented cases (for further information on Fortress Europe, see www.unitedagainstracism.org; for the Mexican–US border see GAO-06–770). The Mediterranean Sea has turned into a cemetery for transgressive travellers, and the floating dead bodies washing up on the shores of European tourist islands are evidence of border-necropolitics. The border regime exercises its power not only through 'the right to live or die' but pre-eminently through 'the right to expose to death' (Mbembe 2003; Perera 2006). The border regime exposes transgressive refugees/travellers to death by consigning them to 'the zones of exemption where the sovereign power cease to function' (Rajaram and Grundy-Warr 2004:38).

Or as Inda puts it, borders do not kill or want immigrants to die but are 'willing to tolerate casualties' (2007:149). Sacrifice is a primary act of worship. Sacrificing border transgressors is part of the worship of the nation-state and acknowledgement of its sovereignty.

Homayoun and I fled from the camp under cover of darkness later that day on the back of a pickup going southward. For fear of the Pakistani military, bandits, 'refugee warriors' (Shahrani 1995), Afghan Mujaheddin and the Red Army, the driver drove very fast over the wastelands. I could barely hold on. The driver advised me that when – and not if – I heard shooting, I should lie flat on the floor of the pickup, as it would reduce my chances of getting shot. Around midnight we crossed the border. The border between Afghanstan and Pakistan was and still is very porous. There were no guards or barriers. A single room, which was supposed to be a check-point, was the only trace of the nation-state system. Homayoun told me later that the Pakistani soldiers leave the border posts at night for fear of being killed by Afghan Mujaheddin or other armed gangs. In many ways, my journey resembles that of the two Afghan youngsters in Michael Winterbottom's drama-documentary *In this World*, though heading in the opposite direction. The pickup kept going all night, and at dawn we reached a small town. It was on the Pakistani side but crammed with Afghan refugees and armed Mujaheddin. The driver said that Red Army jets occasionally bombed the town because of the concentration of Afghans. The town was completely lawless. Homayoun said that all kinds of weapons and drugs were more or less sold openly on the streets. The driver took us to a garage, where I got some rest. Homayoun went away to find out how we could get to Karachi. Around noon, he came back with two bus tickets to Quetta, the largest city in northwestern Pakistan. It was not easy to find a way out of the town, as thousands of refugees were searching for vehicles to take them south to a safer place. After a modest lunch, we went to the bus terminal. The bus, decorated and painted like a holy shrine, was overloaded. Refugees occupied the aisle and a hand-ful of people even sat on its roof. All the other passengers were Afghan refugees. I still wore Afghan clothes and was instructed by Homayoun how to present myself as a Kabuli. I should pretend to be a boy from *Peghman*, an affluent neighbourhood in north Kabul, and say that my father was an export–import merchant and that we had lived for several years in Iran. That would explain my accent. Although *Dari*, a major language of Afghanstan – particularly in northern parts and in Kabul – is Farsi, my dialect would easily disclose my origin.

At sunset, the bus stopped at a mosque for evening prayer. All the passengers went inside. They were Sunni Muslims and I did not know their way of prayer, so I hid myself under the bus until the ceremony had finished. On the bus, Homayoun replaced my white sneakers – which would 'definitely betray me' – with his own more 'ordinary' shoes. All these precautions did not help when a police officer at a checkpoint said, without hesitation, 'You are not Afghan', and asked for my passport. Once again, the border problem was solved with a few rupees. My 'travel contract' with Homayoun included bribes in the price. I heard later from other Iranians that they were forced by their smugglers to pay the bribes themselves. I do not know how much Homayoun bribed the border guards, the bus driver to let me on, the hotel managers to overlook my illegality, and many others. I did, however, witness many people 'earning' money thanks to my journey.

Quetta is the provincial capital and an important political and economic centre due to its location between Afghanistan and Pakistan. It is also linked to Iran by road and railway. This city of one to two million inhabitants (depending on who is counted) has historically been a migrant city. First came Muhajirs, Muslims who migrated to Pakistan from India after independence in 1947, and then Baluchi, Hazaras and Pashtun immigrants, followed by Afghan refugees in the 1980s. There are also a great many Baluchis from Iran. As a real border city, the cultural diversity of Quetta was genuine. Most people spoke several languages, including Urdu, Baluchi, Dari/Farsi and Pastun, and a few could even speak English. I could communicate easily in Farsi. Everywhere I went, Iranian pop music, alongside Indian and Pashtun music, was played loudly in music stores. So-called transnationalism was tangible here, far from the global nodes known for transnationality, such as London, New York and Toronto. In Quetta I was able to take a shower for the first time in many days. I changed my clothes, now torn and dirty, to a new Afghan outfit. The Office of the United Nations High Commissioner for Refugees (UNHCR) in Quetta gave me a letter, which had no legal or political significance. The officer said that they could not do more for me and that, since Quetta was unsafe for Iranian refugees, I should go to Karachi. Outside the office, an Iranian man belonging to the Iranian Peoples' Mujaheddin, a militant group opposed to the Iranian state, asked me to join them. When I refused, he turned to Homayoun and yelled at him that he should rescue 'genuine political refugees' and not people like me. It was the first time, but not the last, that I was told I was not a 'genuine' refugee. This man's notion of a 'real' refugee from Iran was shared by many of the UNHCR officers I met on my journey. Later on that day, I faced more hostility. In a restaurant at the table next to us, a middle-aged Afghan man heard my Farsi accent and began to blame Iranians for discriminating against and mistreating Afghan immigrants in Iran. He was quite right and I told him so. But he was really upset and his voice got louder. All the others in the restaurant, also Afghans, agreed with him. The situation got ugly and the man approached us in a hostile way, but Homayoun intervened and we rushed out.

The journey by land to Karachi is almost 900 kilometres. Taking it would have meant many checkpoints and many people to be bribed, so we decided to travel by air. With the paper I had received from UNHCR, I could obtain a ticket. At Karachi airport we noticed that a police van was following our taxi. The van overtook us after a few kilometres and its occupants ordered the taxi driver to stop. Seven policemen surrounded the taxi, but 500 rupees (approximately USD 40) more and we were again free. I realized later on that this was a rite of passage for all undocumented refugees arriving at Karachi airport. Just before midnight, we arrived in the vicinity of the railway station in central Karachi. Cantt Station was an odd place packed with Iranian, Iraqi and Afghan refugees, together with poor Pakistani migrant workers, petty gangsters, drug dealers, male prostitutes and a sea of beggars. On the eastern side of the railway station, in a triangular block, there were several small, cheap hotels, mostly occupied by Iranian refugees. The lobbies and coffee houses next to the hotels were a sort of 'migration market' where human smugglers met their clients and dealers and middlemen hunted newly arrived refugees. Cantt Station was, in some ways, an urban refugee camp in the larger city. Life there was a horror version of *Casablanca*. There was also an Iranian restaurant and a hostel where Iranians could receive money transfers from Iran. Iranians who lived elsewhere in the city came there to get news and meet other Iranians. Such nodes can be found in all big cities that are transit points for undocumented migrants and refugees. Like Cantt Station in Karachi, there is a park near *Gare de l'est* in Paris, which has been a site for undocumented migrants on their way to England or other countries since the late 1990s. The nodal point for Iranian migrants and refugees in Istanbul was and to some extent still is the Aksaray area (see Yaghmaian 2005). Another significant nodal point for undocumented migrants from Africa and Asia en route to Europe today is Patras, a main port in western Greece.

Homayoun left me the day after our arrival to continue his journey to his beloved in Kabul. I never met him again. I do not know whether he survived the Taliban or the American soldiers. Room 404 in Hotel Shalimar, a cheap, shaky five-storey hotel, became my home for the next eight months. Amongst the cheap food stalls on the pavements, which at night were transformed into sleeping-places for the tired bodies of poor domestic migrant workers, Hotel Shalimar stood, still glamorous with its rosy façade and green windows. At night the alleys around the hotel were lively. For those migrant workers who could afford them, simple beds were placed along the wall every night for one rupee a night. Despite the deafening noise of horns mixed with loud popular music from every corner, and among the never-ending traffic of flâneurs, migrant workers fell asleep in the early evening. Those who could not afford a bed often had to wait until after midnight to find a place on the asphalt where they could sleep. We had much better conditions than the domestic migrants.

The restaurant of Hotel Sun Shine on the other side of the street was a meeting place for Iranians. From early evening until midnight or even later, we strolled around Cantt Station, made new friendships and tried to find a way out of Pakistan. In Cantt Station, I learned a new vocabulary with which to talk about the migration market:

*Dal lal* (literally: broker, dealer): human smuggler
*Pardian* (literally: to jump, to fly): irregular migration by air
*Mosafer* (literally: passenger): undocumented migrant
*Daftarche* (literally: booklet): passport
*Kharidan-e forodgah* (literally: buying the airport): bribing airport
  officials

*Passe sefid* (literally: white passport): original passport, blank and not yet issued

*Passe daraje dou* (literally: second-grade passport): hand-made, photo-copied passport

*Khat* (literally: line): route, itinerary

Almost everyone had the same answer: 'There is no point in going to the UNHCR'. It was commonly believed to be a waste of time. Fleeing a war was not a good enough reason and only 'political' (*siyasi*) cases had a chance. Among the many kinds of brokers in the migration market there were even 'case dealers' who sold 'asylum cases'. In the first days I was offered 'a strong case' with 'guaranteed approval' for a hundred dollars. I made a mistake and did not buy it. My fear of being killed in a horrible war was not 'well-grounded' enough, in the view of the UNHCR officer. According to the 1951 Refugee Convention, one is a 'real' refugee only if one has 'well-founded fear of persecution' due to one's 'race, religion, nationality, political opinion, or membership in a particular social group'. So my application was easily and rapidly rejected. The 'case dealer' laughed at me when I told him that my application had been rejected. He was probably right that it was no use telling the UNHCR the truth.

To have a chance of getting refugee status, one must have the ability to translate one's life story into Eurocentric juridical language and to perform the role expected of a refugee. Like other newcomers to Cantt Station, I was advised to wear dirty clothes when going to the UNHCR for the interview and to look 'sad' and 'profound'.

During my fieldwork among refugees and undocumented migrants in Sweden two decades later, I found that they faced a similar situation (see Khosravi 2006, 2009a, 2010). They also need a 'credible' and 'plausible' narrative. To detect a 'genuine' refugee among all the 'bogus' ones, the applicant undergoes comprehensive and complicated hearings. In seeking the 'truth', the hearing system checks and rechecks facts to find contradictions and inconsistencies in the applicant's narrative. The UNHCR's hearing system was based on the assumption that truth telling is connected with remembering detailed information including dates, numbers, names and faces (Bohmer and Shuman 2008:135). The documentary *Well-Founded Fear* shows how a tiny mistake, for example, saying 'October' in the first interview and 'November' in the second, was enough for an

American immigrations officer to reject an application. At the same time, if the applicant narrates his or her story in detail and if all the dates and names of places and people are perfectly consistent, he or she is suspected of fabricating the case. 'How can you remember all these details so well after so many years?' was a question or rather a comment a friend got from a UNHCR officer in Karachi.

The Eurocentric nature of the hearing system was evidenced by our experiences in several ways. Our lives were embedded in an Iranian culture with different assumptions regarding family relations, kinship labels, the calendar system, what was political and what kind of information was significant. For instance, in the interview, I did not mention my flogging, my father's background or my imprisonment, since I did not consider them relevant. Then when I added them to my case, I was asked by a sceptical officer why I offered the new information afterwards. Some refugees are unwilling to reveal private experiences. Women and men do not usually want to talk about being raped or subjected to other sexual torture with a person they have met for the first time through a translator who may be from the same region or city. The film *Unveiled* illustrates this dilemma very well. An Iranian lesbian does not reveal her real reason for exile (that is, persecution by the Iranian authorities for her sexual orientation) to the male officer and male translator at Frankfurt airport because she is afraid of the consequences it might have for her.

Only those few who could 'translate' their local stories into Eurocentric judicial language had a chance. Those who came first were interviewed first, and their narratives of their 'well-founded fear' set the authenticity benchmark the UNHCR officers used in scrutinizing other asylum seekers. The UNHCR officers used information from previous interviews to check the reliability of others' accounts. They had detailed knowledge of Evin and Ghasr, two prisons in Tehran, and of the most infamous interrogators, their appearance and nicknames.

Henry, a young Iranian–Armenian man who lived in room 308 of Hotel Shalimar, was an activist in an Iranian communist militia, *Cherikhaye Fadaiye Khaleq*, but the UNHCR did not believe him. The reason was a wall painting in a basement corridor of a prison in Isfahan where Henry had been detained for several months before his escape to Pakistan. In his interview, Henry was asked by the UNHCR official to say what was painted on the wall in the corridor, to test his reliability. Henry had not seen such a painting so his application was rejected. How did the UNHCR officer know about the wall painting? How could she or he be sure that there was any painting at all in that corridor? Henry was desperate and did not know what to do. Just a few weeks before my departure from Karachi, one morning when the UNHCR officials arrived in their dark-windowed cars, he poured gasoline on himself and struck a match in front of the UNHCR.

Another friend from Hotel Shalimar whom I lost was Behrooz. He was a young student from Tehran and only three years older than I. After one year in Karachi he decided to go to India. There were rumours that the UNHCR in New Delhi was much more sympathetic towards Iranians. He went to Lahore, the second largest city in Pakistan, near the border with India and only 60 kilometres away from Amritsar, centre of the Sikh religion in India.

It was a cheap but very dangerous way into India. The Pakistani–Indian border was and still is one of the most militarized borders in the world. Besides the military, ethno-religious conflict made the border crossing even more dangerous. Stories circulated among refugees in Cantt Station of how people who tried to cross the border were tortured and killed by local people. People I met later on in India confirmed the rumours. Hoshang, a friend from Hotel Shalimar, was lucky to be saved by the border guards when he was almost murdered by a mob. He spent six months in prison and was finally released through UNHCR efforts. Masoud testified to the extreme brutality of the police towards border transgressors. Behrooz saw no other way – he did not have enough money to try other options. A short phone call from Lahore just before his leaving for the border was the last trace of him.

Karachi itself was not safe for refugees. Refugee spies were everywhere. While Saddam Hussein's agents persecuted and murdered Iraqi refugees, Shiite groups supported by the Iranian state attacked Iranian expatriates, ironically, often right in front of the UNHCR building. The moment the buses stopped and screaming young men attacked refugees with chains and sticks, the UNHCR guards closed the gates in panic. The officers watched the scene from the second floor. In front of the closed doors of the UNHCR building and its guards, staff arrived and left in cars with tinted windows, which were swiftly gone from our sight. As a French anthropologist observed in the refugee camps in Kenya, 'the procession arrives in the refugee camps amid a cloud of dust left by their four-wheel drive vehicles, announcing the daily beginning of the international assistance' (Agier 2008:47).

For those of us in Karachi, like many other refugees around the world today, the UNHCR was available but not accessible or reachable. It reminds me now of Franz Kafka's excellent short story, *Before the Law* (2003 [1914]). Here, the law is a door and before the law sits a gatekeeper. A man from the country seeks the law and wishes to gain entry to the law through the doorway. The gatekeeper says that he cannot pass through at the moment: 'Later maybe, but not now'. The gate stands open, but the gatekeeper assures the man that, room to room, there are many more gatekeepers, each more powerful than the other. The man waits by the door for years until he is about to die. Before his death, he asks the gatekeeper, 'So how is it that in all these years, no one except me has requested entry?' The gatekeeper answered, 'This entrance was assigned only to you, and I'm now going to close it'. The similarity between the situation of the stateless and refugees in front of the UNHCR building and the man from the countryside in Kafka's *Before the Law* is undeniable (see Pratt 2005:212–213; see also Agamben 1998:49–50). Both illustrate the 'abstractness' of the law: its availability in terms of international conventions and declarations, concurrent with its inaccessibility to those who need it. For stateless refugees, law, conventions and declarations are available but not accessible.

Once we were attacked in Cantt Station by a group of Pakistanis. Bahram, my roommate in room 404, was burned on his neck with an unknown liquid. He was on the street when a lorry turned into the neighbourhood. A gang of men shouted things in Urdu and cast small plastic bags of burning liquid at the Iranians. Fortunately, the liquid was not strong and Bahram received only minor injuries to his neck and chest. Going to the police would only have resulted in being robbed. The status of 'illegality' deprived us of protection, either from any state or from the UN. Excluded from the legal system, the 'illegal' migrant is an object for necropolitics, 'exposed to death' (Mbembe 2003).

The irony was that an officer from the Pakistani secret police was placed in Cantt Station to monitor the *refugees'* activities. The secret police officer, who was indeed not secret enough, was around 40 years old and had migrated from a village in northern Pakistan to Karachi. He was friendly and, shortly after his arrival at Cantt Station, we became good companions, sharing our early morning habit of drinking *doudpati* (milk tea) with small crispy 'British' biscuits at the small restaurant beneath Hotel Sun Shine (opposite Hotel Shalimar), where he had a room.

One of our conversations was about the Iranian and Pakistani national airlines, Iran Air and Pakistan International Airlines (PIA). We talked about their airplane models, international flight routes and destinations. In a way, we were each competing for our national airline by asserting it to be the more 'advanced' and more 'modern'. The destinations were, of course, limited almost entirely to European and North American cities. We did not even consider each other's countries 'international' destinations. 'International' was synonymous with the Western world. Over our *doudpati* cups, I, a persecuted and undocumented refugee, and a low-ranking police officer from a village in north Pakistan, in a deplorable and dreadful place of indescribable poverty – packed with refugees and human/narcotic smugglers – 'travelled in the West', to use Amitav Ghosh's words. This famous Indian anthropologist and novelist impressively describes his conversation with an Egyptian Imam about the military capacities of India and Egypt as they discussed which one was more 'advanced' (Ghosh 1986). In the discussion between the Pakistani police officer and me, our countries' links to the West via their national airlines (cf. Ferguson 1999:235) were cited as hallmarks of the modern world. The officer's and my imaginings of fortune, success, being part of the modern world, and our fascination with the West were all undoubtedly common factors that have led to the emergence of current migration patterns. Migrants are not only 'victims' of poverty and conflicts, pushed to leave. Their decision to migrate can also be based on a desire for and fascination with the modern lifestyle of the industrialized world (see Mai 2001; Gebrewold 2007 ). Information, images, myths and stories of success in the West are transmitted through personal networks and the media (Mai 2001). The result is a powerful 'imagination' (Appadurai 1996), creating alternative worlds and lifestyles. In these imaginary stories, however, failure, discrimination, racism and the harsh realities of the life facing immigrants in the West are ignored and held back. Unsurprisingly, disillusionment has been very common among my undocumented informants in Sweden, for whom Sweden had been associated with generosity, hospitality and democracy.

Summer arrived and the heat had already become unbearable by late April. No hotel in Cantt Station was air-conditioned and the hot breeze from a slowly whirling ceiling fan was all we had. In the afternoons, the heat drove us to the comfort of the air-conditioned library of the American Consulate. After we went through security control, in the calm and breezy lounge, we, who had not slept the night before because of the heat, occupied couches and comfy chairs to take a nap. The consulate was located next to a luxury hotel and a modern business complex. Only a park divided us from them. On one side of the park there were authorized well-to-do people in a cosmopolitan scene: an international chain hotel, consulates, offices of multinational companies, travel agencies and language schools. On the other side, alongside poor domestic migrants, we were condemned to an agonizing immobility.

Since there were no telephones in the rooms of Hotel Shalimar, communication with Iran was not easy. Our families called the reception and anyone of us who happened to be around paged the person. If the person was not inside the hotel, one of us talked to his parents to deliver a message. Many of us, the guests of Hotel Shalimar, got to know each other's families. In some cases, our parents even met each other in Iran to exchange information and support each other in transferring money or finding a way out of Pakistan. The usual way of communication was mail. I never forget the first letter I received from Iran, around two months after my arrival in Karachi, in late April. In the small lobby of the hotel, Pour, a young Iranian man with whom I shared room, handed me a letter that had arrived that day. It was from my mother. I left the hotel and went to the park, the border between our world and the cosmopolitan one. In the middle of this 'no man's land', amid a transient and erratic life, my mother's handwriting raised in me a sense of hominess. On the back of the letter my father, to give me courage, wrote how we Bakhtiaris have survived generations of natural, political and social crisis. He reminded me of his and my time in prison, how his grandparents and my mother's had been persecuted in the early twentieth century by the state, and how his property had been confiscated both before and after the Revolution. He simply asked me to be a *man*, like himself, strong and brave. But in that park, at a time of disconnect-edness, disruption and migrant illegality, I just wished to be home.

To kill time in the long and tedious afternoons, I started to draw a map of Isfahan on a large sheet of paper. Maps of Iranian cities were unavailable in Karachi at that time. I drew details, with names of streets, alleys, parks, cafés, schools, bookstores and shopping malls of which I had memories. There were four Isfahanis in the hotel. At night, we went over the map and talked about Isfahan. For the first time in my life, I felt attachment to that city.

There were many *dal lals* (literally: brokers) – or, as they are usually called, human smugglers – in Cantt Station, from big ones like Nasser, the Baluch who had hundreds of *mosafer*s (travellers, clients), to small amateurs. Many smugglers were themselves migrants or refugees who engaged in the business for a few years before going to the West. In addition, there were a large number of dealers, middlemen and lackeys who worked for the smugglers. The smugglers usually demanded all or much of the payment in advance. When this was paid, they let hell loose on their clients. Young women might be sexually abused for long periods before the smugglers sent them on. Sometimes smugglers forced their clients to be drug carriers, to take 'a bag' with them to Europe. Young men were turned into lackeys who would hunt new clients. Alireza was one of them. He was the first one who befriended me in Cantt Station. The day after my arrival, I met him in the restaurant of Hotel Sun Shine. He came to my table and gave me information about the 'situation'. Alireza was a talented and lovely boy. His first smuggler disappeared with his and probably many others' money and his second one went into bankruptcy. Alireza changed gradually. He began to collect clients for his smuggler in the hope that, with the newcomers' money, the smuggler might pay him back. As far as I know, he remained in Karachi for many years.

There was no *dal lal* in our hotel, except for Farhad. He called him-self a smuggler but in fact, he was nothing more than a dealer for the big smugglers. In room 304, right under my room, Farhad lived with two Iranian teenagers, a brother and sister. The sister was a few years older than her brother. The siblings had given all their money to Farhad to be smuggled to Canada. It was obvious to all that Farhad had no intention of sending the teenagers anywhere, or of returning their money. The situation became worse when he moved into their room. After that, the girl never left the room. There were rumours that Farhad was sexually abusing her. How could they protest? Farhad had all the money their parents had saved to send them to safety. Before our very eyes, Farhad was holding them captive. Once, a few of us gave him a beating. Yet nothing changed. He stayed in the siblings' room for many months. We could have done more to help them, but we did not. To relieve my shame, I used to remind myself that we were undocumented, scared young men in our late teenage years. But it does not help. The shame is unavoidable. Room 304 in Hotel Shalimar is still a frequent nightmare.

## Border, gender and sexuality

Borders are not only racialized; they are also pre-eminently gendered and sexualized. However, the gender and sexual aspects of migration studies have traditionally been restricted to focusing on family relationships, the household (Luibhéid 2004), transnational motherhood or human trafficking for the sex industry (with the exception of Luibhéid 2002, Cantú et al. 2009). One sexual aspect of borders is the rape of border crossers. Women and, to a lesser extent, men run the risk of being raped not only by bandits and smugglers but also by border guards. Rape at borders is systematic, occurs routinely and follows a similar pattern along borders in different places. Rape has become a mechanism of border control. On the Mexico–USA border, rape has been routinely used by the state in its efforts to militarize the border (Falcón 2001, 2007; Carpenter 2006). Although the outcome is the same for its victims, rape on the border differs from rape in war or in prison (Falcón 2001:32). It is not a strategy for defeating the enemy or even a sort of punishment. It is instead a border 'tariff', and border transgressors are raped to get permission to cross. After being raped by the border guards, Mexican women are allowed to continue their journey into the USA (Falcón 2001:34). The rape of Mexican women as the price of safe passage to *el norte* is an old custom (Martínez 1998:58). Unsurprisingly, women en route to the USA use birth control pills, since they anticipate the possibility of rape.

Rape in exchange for safe passage is a 'rite of passage' many border crossers face at various borders (Wali 1990; Human Rights Watch 1995; Luibhéid 2002:129). Some undocumented women migrants from Central America to the USA pay higher fees to the *coyotes* for 'additional protection' (Hagan 2008). Being raped is also the price of receiving the necessary documents. In *Casablanca*, the newly-married Bulgarian woman is asked by the police chief to sleep with him if she wants to get an exit visa. The Iranian woman in *The Guests of Hotel Astoria* is raped by a Turkish officer before being allowed to leave Turkey. The young woman residing in room 304 of Hotel Shalimar shared her bed with her smuggler to find a way out of her exile hell. Sexual abuse and harassment may even continue long after migrants have crossed the border. Undocumented migrants and asylum seekers are vulnerable groups targeted for sexual abuse. Undocumented Burmese women in Thailand are recurrently raped by gangs who say that they will avoid arrest since the women are 'illegal migrants' (*The Irrawaddy*, 20 October 2008).

The 'impunity' of the rapists and their lack of accountability to the authorities reveal the patriarchal modus operandi of the nation-state system, based on the conflation of militarized masculinity and so-called national securitization. Female asylum seekers in Western countries have been asked for sexual services by immigration officers in exchange for resolving their asylum problems (Luibhéid 2002:129). In Sweden, an officer at the Migration Board visited several female applicants outside working time, had pictures of them on his cell phone, and asked them for sexual services in exchange for assistance in their asylum process (Swedish Radio, 21 January 2008). Several undocumented migrants I met during my research had similar experiences. Bahman, an Iranian man in his late twenties, was forced to give sexual services to his landlady under the threat of being reported to the police. Another young and handsome Iranian man, Hamid, reluctantly had sex with his lawyer for one year for fear that she would otherwise diminish his chances of regularization. Pari, an Iranian woman in her mid-thirties, hoped for regularization through marriage; she entered into a relationship with a man and was 'with him' at the weekends for two years.

Rape at the border is not intended to keep migrant women *out* but rather to keep them *in their places* in terms of the racial and gender hierarchy (Carpenter 2006:174). As Luibhéid states (2002), rape is not a strategy for keeping migrants out, but rather a method for reproducing hierarchical social relationships, in which female *citizens* are 'pure' and border transgressors are regarded as rapable. Rape reproduces borders.

Furthermore, borders are based on heterosexual norms. Some borders target homosexuals (Stychin 2000; Luibhéid 2004, 2008 ). For example, in many states same-sex couples are essentially excluded from reunification policies, since they cannot use their relationships as a basis for legal immigration. Borders also target victims of trafficking for the sex industry and other industries (see van den Anker and Doomernik 2006), by deporting them to countries where they face the poverty they fled or most likely debts to their traffickers. They are doubly punished, first by the trafficker and then by the Western states.

Pakistan in the mid-1980s was wracked by political instability. The president was General Muhammad Zia-ul-Haq, who had seized power in a military coup d'état in 1977 against the ruling Prime Minister Zulfikar Ali Bhutto (who was later executed). The Soviet invasion of Afghanstan, the immigration of millions of Afghan refugees, Islamization and undemocratic elections resulted in turbulence throughout the 1980s. Violent confrontations, political riots and terrorism were increasing in Pakistan's large cities in 1987 and soared with the assassination of General Zia-ul-Haq on 17 August 1988. In response to a series of terror actions, Pakistan sharpened its border control. Throughout the spring and summer of 1987, no one I knew from Cantt Station succeeded in leaving Pakistan by air. The police had stopped collaborating with smugglers and those who tried anyway ended up in jail. Moreover, the *khats* (literally: line, flight route) from Karachi to Europe had been discovered by European police and many migrants were being deported back to Karachi. Karachi had become a blind alley. We could not find a way out.

Once in a restaurant in Cantt Station I was drinking *doudpati* with a well-known *dal lal*, a middle-aged man from a prominent Baluchi clan. I told him about my desperate situation and that I was pessimistic about being able to leave Pakistan. He smiled and said in heavily accented Farsi: 'My son, the world's door cannot be closed' (*dar-e donya ra nemishe bast*). Amir Heidari, perhaps the best-known *dal lal* in the Middle East and Europe in the 1980s and the 1990s, whom I interviewed in prison in Sweden in May 2004 and June 2009, used another figure of speech: 'It is like running water. If you put a stone in its way, you might stop it for a while but it soon finds another course'.

My *dal lal* was Abbas, a second-generation Iranian immigrant in Karachi. In his early thirties, Abbas was a businessman with a 'good' reputation in the Iranian immigrant community. His parents had immigrated to Pakistan in the 1950s. His father established a business and opened an Iranian restaurant, which was now run by Abbas. He promised to send me to a European country for USD 2500. Two months or so after my arrival in Karachi, my father paid the money to Abbas's brother-in-law in Iran. Several times I saw Iranian diplomats eating with him in a corner of his restaurant. This frightened me, and I told him that I had changed my plans and asked for my money back. Arguing that he had already paid for a passport, which I never saw, and other expenses he said, 'Wait a little longer, I will send you soon'. This was a usual trick used by the smugglers, keeping the client hoping. Weeks passed and I realized that Abbas had no intention of arranging my journey. I asked him again to return my money. He refused and said, 'I will send you. Come back next week'. This 'come back next week' was repeated for a further four months.

Abbas was a giant, with curly black hair, thick eyebrows and a big moustache. He never threatened me directly, but his lackeys, a handful of Pakistani men, did. Furthermore, a few police officers visited his restaurant occasionally. I found myself completely powerless. Abbas was an influential businessman with connections with the police and the Iranian consulate. I did not even have a passport. While the secret police monitored us as threats, people smugglers (with our money) mingled freely with diplomats and the police.

Unable to demand my money back, I embarked on a new strategy. As a businessman, Abbas needed to keep his good reputation. One day I stood in front of his restaurant from the time it opened until one or two in the morning when it closed. I did this again and again. At first, he ignored me. Then his workers threatened me and pushed me away. But I was there the next day – I had no other way out. Once, at the weekend, when Abbas, along with his parents, sister, wife and children came to eat in the restaurant, I stood at the door and told them my story and asked them to intervene. Abbas was upset and I was dragged away by his workers. His father became upset and said that it was my own fault. Soon after that night, however, Abbas gave me back USD 2000 and said that the remaining USD 500 had been paid for a false passport that he refused to give me.

One week later, in late October, I left Karachi for Delhi – in our jargon, I *paridam* (jumped, flew). After eight months in Cantt Station, I knew exactly what to do. It was impossible for me to make it to Europe by myself, so I decided to go to India. For USD 500 I bought an Iranian passport, the owner of which had already been smuggled to Europe, probably using a European passport. It had belonged to a young woman, named Shahrzad, but in that sort of Iranian passport the owner's gender was not indicated. Passports had a price. She was probably able to get a discount by letting the smuggler keep her passport for another client.

An Iranian–Armenian, famous for his high-quality work in forging stamps and 'doctoring' photos, replaced the owner's photo with mine. He was a painter and in his room in central Karachi he had some of his works hanging on the wall. This artist was probably on his way to the West, and doctoring photos was a way to save up for a passport and a ticket. He also put the necessary stamps – such as a false entry stamp to Pakistan – in the passport. Then an Afghan dealer got me a genuine visa to India for USD 500. He also arranged a contact at the Karachi airport for a few hundred dollars. I obtained the ticket from a travel agency in Cantt Station. The agency demanded something like USD 50 or USD 60 to ignore my situation. Everyone wanted a piece of the cake.

I paid my debts to my friends and to Mr Karim, the manager of Hotel Shalimar, who had kindly let me stay on credit. I said goodbye to only a few 'friends' in the hotel, as there was a rule, 'Do not trust even your brother'. The first advice I got in Karachi was a Farsi expression saying: 'Sleep far from Iranians and you won't have nightmares' (*dor az irani bekhab, khabe ashofte nabin*). Incidents like friends or roommates cheating each other for money or stealing travel documents were not unusual. In Cantt Station you never knew who was friend and who was foe. Rival smugglers would inform the airport authorities to damage each other's business. For stateless refugees secrecy is vital.

In the evenings when we, the guests of Hotel Shalimar, gathered in the lobby or outside the hotel, sitting on the pavement, where guests of other hotels joined us, we could guess who had left us that day. When the person was safe somewhere else in the world, his friend or roommate would let us know the details of that person's *paridan* (jump, flight). Every single detail of a successful 'jump' was valuable to those of us left behind.

At the Karachi airport, the immigration officer who was bribed to let me through asked me to follow him to his office. There he asked me to put all I had on the table. He was robbing me. Since I had expected such, I had hidden a USD 100 bill, all I had left, inside my belt. I put a USD 20 bill I had set aside for this situation on the table. He got upset and asked for more money. When I said I had no more, he pointed to the chain that I had worn since I was a child, a keepsake from my mother. I refused, vehemently and loudly. First, he threatened me but then he took the USD 20 bill and let me go. I was robbed twice at Karachi airport, once on arrival by the police and once by an immigration officer when leaving.

# 3
# The Community of Displacement

At Delhi airport, an Iranian woman who saw the brown-coloured Iranian passport in my hand asked me to help her to fill out a customs form. When finished, I told her that I was travelling 'illegally', so it was better for her not to be seen with me. She got worried and left me but waited for me on the other side of the border. The Armenian artist had forged my passport professionally and I, or rather Shahrzad, went through border control without any problem. The Iranian woman and I shared a taxi to New Delhi. She was visiting her son, who had been living clandestinely in Delhi for a long time. It was almost midnight when we arrived downtown, and she kindly let me stay the night at their place. Her son shared a room with another young man. Although there was barely enough space for themselves, she graciously told me that I could stay with them as long as I wanted. Her hospitality was unconditional, and she did not expect to be repaid or even to see me again. The journey would have been impossible to accomplish without the hospitality of the many strangers I met en route. Her son told me I could find Iranians in the Defence Colony market – a smaller and more upscale version of Cantt Station.

In the next few days, I visited the neighbourhood to find a contact. Defence Colony, in the centre of New Delhi, was a relatively leafy middle-class neighbourhood squeezed between three huge motorways. The inhabitants of the neighbourhood were mainly retired military officers, mostly Sikhs, who rented their servants' rooms to undocumented migrants. It was a remarkable community composition. The local market, in the north part of the neighbourhood, was a 100-metre-long street lined with small shops and restaurants pressed against each other on both sides, with a small green median running down the middle. Besides a Chinese restaurant and a hamburger stand, there was a small eating-place where we could get tasty *masala dosa*, a popular Indian crêpe, for a few rupees.

There were a lot of Iranians, but I did not know any of them. I had already spent some of my hundred dollars and I did not know when I would receive more money from Iran. To save money, I slept in a small park at the edge of Defence Colony. It was in fact a green space, as large as a block, with a few metal benches. Although the neighbourhood was relatively safe, I was worried about being robbed. Changed into Indian currency, the 100-dollar bill had become a large sum of money. I hid it in different places, mostly in my shoes. In my small bag, the one I brought from Iran, I had a few pieces of clothing, a toothbrush, the map of Isfahan I drew in Hotel Shalimar, and several pictures my friends and family had sent me when I was in Pakistan. The first night in the park, I looked at the pictures. They had been taken after my departure and showed parties and weddings. One of them was taken at a cousin's wedding. It was probably late and taken when all other guests had already left the party. Almost all my cousins were in the pictures, laughing into the camera. Most likely many of them were drunk. On the back of the picture, my sister had written a Farsi expression: 'Your place was empty' (*jat khali bod*).

Maybe one day I will forget my name, but not that first night in the park, in southern New Delhi in October 1987. When night had settled in and midnight approached, when fewer and fewer people were around and the silence had become more intense, when not even holy cows could be seen, when the lights in the houses around the park were turned off one after the other, when the nightly stillness was only broken occasionally by passing auto-rickshaws, a fatal sense of solitude seeped into every cell of my body. Then my loneliness was at its most definite, tangible.

Our family had two big houses, one in Isfahan and one in Khanemirza, and their doors were always open to friends and strangers. Everyone from our region in the Bakhtiari who came to Isfahan stayed at our home. Old people came to visit the doctor, parents to purchase dowries for their daughters, young people to seek jobs, others to consult my father about local conflicts, and young women for prenatal care. Some stayed a few nights, some several months. We all became involved in our guests' affairs. While we children helped with translation or acted as city guides, my mother negotiated with doctors, hospitals or retailers. We were involved in our guests' happiness and suffering. In summertime, when we were in Khanemirza, people from Isfahan and Tehran came to spend time in what was for them an exotic landscape. I remember that sometimes we did not even know our guests. They might be cousins of my sister's teacher, or travellers who had got lost. Now and then, we children would complain that we had no privacy, but my mother used to say that the worst person in the Bakhtiari was the one whose home was closed to others (*dar-e khone baste*). Hospitality, for her, was not just a polite gesture, a sign of nobility, but the very essence of being human. I never told her about my nights in the park – how could I?

After a few days, I got to know Hiva, a middle-aged undocumented Afghan prostitute who usually hung around the Defence Colony market waiting for customers. I met her for the first time at the hamburger stand. She had been a dancer in Kabul before she was forced to flee because of her occupation. One aspect of border crossing is anonymity and the absence of the social moral codes, as borderlands are 'tolerant zones' for 'immoral activities'. The Mexico–USA border has been such a 'tolerant zone', where American and Mexican gay men can escape strict moral mores (Cantú 2002).

G.B. Road, the red-light district in New Delhi, was crammed with Nepalese prostitutes. From windows on the second floor of shabby buildings on both sides of the street, in colourful saris, women of all ages, many with small children, invited passing men to buy leisure or tenderness. The money they sent home cured a sick father, paid for children's education or provided food for an unemployed husband. Borderlands offer sites for work that may not be acceptable in the homeland. Hiva refused to talk to me in our common language, Farsi/Dari, but preferred to speak English. Perhaps in a foreign language, in a borderland, she found it easier to be a prostitute. For many people, crossing borders by migrating provides the space and 'permission' to cross boundaries and transform their sexuality and sex roles (Espín 1999:5). Crossing borders confers the freedom to invent new lifestyles and schemes of self-representation (Stychin 2000).

Nevertheless, Hiva was not safe from harassment in Defence Colony. Many Afghan refugees saw her as a disgrace to their nation.

She was fearful when she saw a fellow countryman, for whom her body was a bearer of Afghan masculine identity, of men's honour and the motherland. Her sexual shame offended their sense of honour. Marginalized even in her own ethnic community, she suffered from a double marginality. Just as an anthropologist in a new field is first contacted and helped by the most marginalized members of the society, Hiva was the first one who saw me, who accepted me. We two deviants, one a prostitute and one a stateless refugee, easily found each other. One day Hiva told me that she had heard that a man from the Bakhtiari lived in Defence Colony. I went to the address and met Fariborz, a middle-aged man who lived with six other Iranian refugees in a little room. They did not hesitate a second to share their room, which was barely enough even for themselves, with me. We had access to a little toilet next to the room and went to a nearby sports stadium to shower. We cooked simple food on some primitive equipment we had in the corner of the room. Sleeping-places were well organized so everybody could stretch out without bothering anyone else.

Despite the overcrowded conditions and poor food, I have many pleasant memories of my life in New Delhi. I gradually got to know other Iranians in Defence Colony. Compared with Cantt Station, Defence Colony was heaven. At least we were safe from police robbery and brutality against refugees. I sent letters to Hotel Shalimar and described the situation in India. Several Hotel Shalimar guests arrived after me, coming to India by train, foot or air. All ended up in Defence Colony.

The good times in Defence Colony came to an end one night when the 'Colonel', our landlord, an elegant retired army officer, found out that up to eight people were living in the room, not just the two to whom he had rented it. We were immediately evicted. We moved to a four-bedroom apartment in Noida, a suburb in Southeastern New Delhi. To afford the rent, we shared the apartment with two Iranian refugee families, making 16 of us, including four children. For a short time, Sassan's mother also lived with us. With all the children and parents around, I remember the time in Noida as one of homeliness. At night, Amir read Farsi poetry to us or Reza played guitar and sang nostalgic songs. In late fall, it got cold and we had nothing with which to warm our rooms. Sometimes the severe cold forced us to gather around the gas cooker in the kitchen.

However, in New Delhi my situation improved dramatically. There was no police harassment and it was easier to move around in the huge city. During my five months in New Delhi, I shared rooms with many people in transit. Most of them are now residents of Europe or North America – thanks to the *dal lals*, smugglers (see Appendix). The rumour in Karachi was correct. The UNHCR in New Delhi was much more humane: the personnel were helpful and the building was more welcoming, in contrast to the fortress-like one in Karachi. I was recognized as a person in need of protection but, unlike in Karachi, the UNHCR offered no resettlement programme, that is, migration to a safe third country for permanent residence. Instead, I got a 'refugee card' and USD 50 a month. It was just enough to pay for my share of the rent and for two weeks of food. The rest I received from Iran.

Transferring money from Iran to India was very difficult. The formal money transfer channels were blocked because of the war, so informal ones were the only option. Unlike Karachi, there was no Iranian immigrant community in New Delhi. Those who had relatives in the USA or Europe received money easily through the banking system, but not us whose money came from Iran. After a month or so in New Delhi, my father sent money via an Indian man who arrived from Tehran. He had been a Sikh immigrant in Iran for decades and a successful businessman. Through personal networking, my father had come in contact with him. Nevertheless, he gave me a few hundred dollars less than my father had paid him, arguing that 'it costs'. In the informal life, everything costs. We 'illegal' travellers were an easy source of income for many people we came across en route. Having someone – a sibling, friend or even distant relative – in Europe, Canada or the USA meant a lot to refugees. Having such a network meant security and self-confidence. Besides economic support, the network meant access to information and having a clear and defined prospect of one's eventual journey.

There is agreement among migration scholars that social networks, based on kinship, friendship and community ties, are central to migration systems (Boyd 1989; see also Gurak and Caces 1992). Social networks facilitate migration by providing financial support and information. They substantially reduce the risk and cost of migration (Massey 1986). Since each new migrant creates his or her own networks, the range of social connections expands, making subsequent migration easier. Accordingly, network expansion leads to more migration, which in turn leads to further network expansion. Over time, networks establish a self-perpetuating cycle that underlies chain migration. Migration becomes a self-sustaining social enterprise and continues independently of its original causes (Massey 1986:112). Social networks facilitate ongoing migration flow and increase the likelihood of others at home joining their compatriots abroad (Papadopoulou 2008:84). The social relations and psychological factors influencing migration decisions often determine the direction of migration movements as well as their extent (Talpos et al. 2008). The country of destination was primarily determined by such networks. The present Iranian diaspora is only three decades old. The 1979 revolution and the outbreak of the Iran–Iraq war caused a huge emigration of Iranians, both voluntary and involuntary, to Western countries. Accordingly, no 'migration industry' existed in the 1980s. The prior migrant population in Western countries was still small and migration networks were primarily based on family connections. Today there is a large well-established migration industry in operation in the Iranian transnational diasporic community. Through network-mediated migration, Iranians today can move faster, easier and more purposefully than before. For those of us who lacked access to such migration networks, decisions were made under conditions of uncertainty and migration more or less followed a trajectory of wandering.

Religion, like ethnicity, may offer a form of social capital that people use when migrating. Religion as an aspect of the migration process has been overlooked in migration and particularly irregular migration studies (exceptions are Koser Akcapar 2006; Hagan 2008 ). In Karachi and New Delhi, our religious identities made a huge difference to our destinies. Iranians of Christian faith, mainly Armenians and Assyrians, had a chance to resettle in the USA. Iranian Jews could enjoy *aliyah*, the right of return to Israel. Baha'is had access to well-established transnational networks that helped them escape persecution in Iran. For some Iranian Muslims, conversion to Christianity became a migration strategy. Conversion also meant access to new local social networks, such as churches and church-related organizations (see Koser Akcapar 2006). Hagan (2008) has observed how faith helps migrants cope with the traumas and uncertainties they face en route. As a protecting and guiding force, religion can play a crucial role in the wandering trajectory of migrants, such as Frank.

## Biographical vignette

### Frank in Istanbul

In December 2005 I was in Istanbul attending a conference on irregular migration to Europe. On the second day, I left the conference to visit my favourite neighbourhood, Tophane. It is located on the European side of the Bosphorus, filled with overcrowded multi-storey buildings from the Ottoman era on both sides of narrow alleys. White sheets and clothes hanging on rotary clotheslines decorate the laneways with colour and compensate for the worn façades of the houses. Tophane is always full of intergenerational life, and the noise of children playing is ceaseless. While old and middle-aged men occupy the cafés, drinking tea and smoking water pipes, women sit chatting in the windows and doorways, and there are cats everywhere. Strolling with no intention of going back to the conference, in one of the cross alleys a small but beautiful Gothic-style church caught my eye, hidden behind old trees and greenery. Heading towards it, I saw two men in front of the church, the younger probably African while the other had a South Asian look. When I approached them to ask about the church, the younger man hurried inside. The older one kindly asked me if I wanted to look around the garden. He asked where I came from and, hearing my answer, switched from English to Farsi. On that sunny afternoon, on a bench in the churchyard, I enjoyed a long conversation with Frank, a Christian Farsi-speaking undocumented Pakistani in Istanbul.

Frank was born in 1952 in a small village in the Gujarat region of eastern Pakistan. Like most of the village population, Frank was born Catholic. He had a tough childhood. His mother died when he was a teenager and his father was a postman whose salary could barely feed Frank and his five brothers. They suffered from a double exclusion: being poor and being non-Muslim. Despite all odds, Frank built up a life for himself in the village. After high school, he studied and worked as a medical technician in a Christian hospital. He began saving for a house, got married and gradually his family grew. Frank has six children, the youngest 11 years old and the oldest 21. Frank was active in his church and acted as a social worker for other Catholic people in need. As a religious minority, the Catholics in Pakistan have always been harassed and discriminated against by the majority Muslims. In the 1990s, however, the situation turned ugly for Christians in Pakistan, particularly in rural areas. His village was regularly attacked by Muslim mobs. Their appeals to the police and the authorities for protection were ignored. The church was burnt down and many people were killed. In desperation and hopelessness, the Bishop committed suicide. Frank himself had been shot with three bullets, and he showed me where they had maimed his body. 'We were told that Pakistan was only for Muslims'. Frank, like many other Christians, decided to leave Pakistan. His plan was to leave alone first; after he had found a safe place, his family would join him. With the help of a friend, who was from the border region, he illegally entered Iran in May 1998. He lived clandestinely in Tehran in five years, working as a construction worker and sending money to his family. Because of his legal situation, his family could not join him. His intention was to bring up his children in a Christian country. In 2004, he paid USD 500 and was smuggled to Turkey. It was more difficult to find work in Istanbul than in Tehran, so he asked the Church for help. We had smoked many cigarettes in the garden before a priest called him inside. I promised him I'd come back the next day to join them in Sunday mass. So the next day, again avoiding the conference, I went back to the church. The ceremony started at 10 o'clock. There were around 30 people, almost all, as Frank told me later, undocumented migrants or refugees from Africa and South Asia. The priest's sermon was about refugees and why the Church has to assist them. The need was apparently mutual – the church would have been completely empty without the migrants. Before I left the church for the airport, Frank asked me if I could give him €500. He needed that money to be smuggled to Greece. He knew an Iranian smuggler who could send him by land. The Turkey–Greece border is a heavily militarized border and unauthorized border crossing entails great risk. I did not know what to do. I gave him my telephone number and some money I had in my wallet. When I embraced him to bid farewell, he started crying.

From Stockholm, I called the church several times to get news of Frank, without result. One year later, in November 2006, I went back to Istanbul to attend a workshop. After checking in at the hotel, I jumped into a cab and went to Tophane to find Frank. The chances of finding a migrant like Frank in the same place after one year were poor. He was presumably already in Greece. The gate of the church was closed. I rang the bell. A young man, probably from a Western African country, came out from behind the closed gate and asked me what I wanted. He was suspicious and vigilant. I said I was looking for Frank. He hesitated at first but went inside the church; after a while, Frank came out. I was glad to see him again, but seeing him in the same situation after a year made me sad. With a big smile on his face, he hugged me. Through a door to the right of the main church entrance we went into the building. We passed through a long, narrow corridor to the back of the main hall where, in a small room, I met several other young men. Frank said that he and 11 other undocumented migrants, seven from Sri Lanka and four from Burundi, lived in that room. Apart a simple cooker, some stew pans and a few bags, the room was bare. A few mattresses and pieces of cardboard covered the stone floor. It was cold. Frank said that they did not pay rent but they had to work to pay for food. Hearing that I was living in Sweden, the men gathered around me and asked about Sweden, whether they had a chance of getting asylum, how they could get there, whether I knew this cousin or that uncle who lived in Stockholm, whether or not Swedes liked refugees, and many other questions, in search of hope, in search of home. Almost everyone mentioned that they had heard that Swedish asylum policy was 'humane' and 'generous'. Many asked for my telephone number and I was glad to give them all the visiting cards I had with me. When I asked them if they were willing to be interviewed individually, they all gave the same answer: 'the Father's permission first'. Unfortunately, the Father was sick and unreachable even though he lived in the church annex.

A man (himself a refugee from Burundi), whom I later realized was the father's 'assistant', could not conceal his irritation at my presence when he entered the room. He yelled at Frank in front of us, asking why he had taken me inside the church. Frank later explained that the situation had been critical for Christians in Istanbul since the Danish Cartoon Affair. Christians had been attacked and threatened in Turkey, and a priest had even been murdered. The man said that the Father would really get angry when he heard that Frank had taken a stranger inside. Apparently, the church strictly controlled the migrants. I felt there was a patronizing relationship between the church and the migrants, resembling the relationship I experienced between undocumented migrants and asylum seekers and the International Federation of Iranian Refugees (IFIR) in Sweden. IFIR, an organization affiliated with the Worker–Communist Party of Iran, assists migrants while at the same time using them for its own political purposes. In the cases of both the church and IRIR, a kind of identity was imposed on the migrants.

Worried about making Frank's situation worse than it already was, I suggested taking a walk. After 20 minutes or so we were on the Galata Bridge. Along the full length of the bridge, underneath it were restaurants and cafés crammed with tourists and joyful young Turks. By now it was already dark. We chose a less crowded café and ordered two coffees. I asked him whether he had had lunch. 'Egg', he said, 'everything else is expensive'. The most usual meal for us in Hotel Shalimar was egg, carrot marmalade, butter and bread. Frank said that when he did not have money enough to buy eggs or bread, he got some food from his roommates, one day from the Sri Lankans, other days from the Burundis.

'They are young and can find work easily. Now and then, there is work for me, too. A Turkish man calls me when a container has arrived and must be unloaded'. His wage for one day of work, about ten hours, was USD 10; for the same work, Turkish workers got USD 60 each. Frank got even less than the other undocumented migrants because employers believed that 'he was old and could not work as hard as the others'. He did not make enough money to send to his family in Pakistan, where his wife also took care of his old father. Frank missed them and cried every time we talked about his children. He had not seen them in eight years and the prospects of reuniting with them in the near future were poor. I asked him what he wanted to do. He said first that he needed money to go to Greece and then to France, but then he said that he did not know what he wanted any more.

The café was now crammed with people. Frank was worried someone would hear what he was saying, so we left the café. Poor people, Turks, migrants and refugees were fishing on the bridge, some for sale, others to get themselves a meal. Vendors, with items like toys, pens, band-aids or combs mounted on cardboard, kept one eye on the passing people and the other on the lookout for police. Suddenly, one peddler started running, probably after seeing policemen, and after him all the others gathered their things and ran away, trying to keep their wares in their arms.

In September 2008, I was back in Istanbul for a workshop on exile. I went to the church, but Frank was not there. The priest said that Frank was still in Istanbul and sometimes attended Sunday mass, but he did not have an address for him.

Ten years after leaving his village, Frank still is in transit, undocumented and seeking a way to get himself to the shores of Europe, where he believed he could reunite with his family. Frank's last words to me on the Galata Bridge that November night in 2006 still ring in my ears: 'I search for light; now my life is dark'.

### Dal lals

With only the money in my hands, I decided to leave India and go on my way. In New Delhi there were a few *dal lals* (smugglers) with good reputations, two of whom were better known than the others. One was Pooya, a young Iranian in his early thirties, a graduate in civil engineering from a university in Delhi, and the other was Nour, a middle-aged Afghan man who lived with his elderly mother in Defence Colony. One day in December 1987 when I went to Nour's place to ask about the rates, his mother invited me in and asked me to stay for lunch. During negotiations over rates, destinations and routes, we were served tasty Afghan food. Nour's mother joined us after lunch and, while preparing tea on a samovar, turned to her son and asked him to give me a discount. Nour told me that his wife and son lived in Canada and he would join them when he had saved enough money to start a business. His mother's hospitality and kindness alongside Nour's reputation for being reliable and proficient made it easy for me to choose him. The rates were not fixed: they increased by the week and sometimes by the day. Like shares, the price of an 'illegal' journey depends on global politics and events. For instance, the death of the President of Pakistan, Muhammad Zia ul-Haq, in a plane crash in August 1988, caused the rates to soar in a day. Furthermore, when a *khat* (literally: line, flight route) was 'discovered' the smuggler would raise the price, arguing that the bribes had increased at the airports and that the routes, flights, transit points and destinations should be changed.

Nour always worked with just a handful of *mosafer* (literally: passengers, clients), and only when they were sent abroad would he take on new ones. In mid-January 1988, I became his *mosafer*. For most European countries, Nour demanded between USD 2300 and USD 2500. By then I had only USD 2000 left of the money my father had sent. Just like any other market negotiation, hard bargaining resulted in a discount of USD 300. Nour gave me two options: The Netherlands or Sweden. I chose The Netherlands. Why? I do not know. Maybe because I had heard more about The Netherlands than about Sweden in my life. The choice of destination was rarely planned. I had no clear image of either of these countries. Nour agreed to send me to The Netherlands for USD 2000 but without 'guarantee', meaning that in case of deportation or arrest he had no obligation towards me. A 'guarantee' cost a few hundred more, which I could not afford.

The destination was determined by the payment. A few hundred dollars could change the destination from one continent to another. Masoud, a roommate, was Nour's *mosafer* (client) at the same time as I was. He had USD 500 more than I did and today he is a Canadian citizen, lives in Toronto and his children's mother tongue is English. I am a Swedish citizen, live in Stockholm and my children's language is Swedish. USD 500 shaped our lives very differently.

Although the payment was crucial, it was not the only factor determining the country of destination. Information or rather rumours concerning the asylum policies of different countries were also a determining factor. Information came from smugglers but also from friends and roommates who had been sent to Europe or Canada. By phone and letter, they sent detailed information about the country of destination, route, airports and journey. For instance, we were informed that France and England had very restrictive policies and that it was almost impossible to get asylum in Italy. Rumour had it that Germany had a generous asylum policy but that, due to the huge flow of asylum seekers to that country, the routes were strictly controlled. Sometimes we were told, 'Do not go to this or that country – all asylum seekers are deported from there. Wait longer'. Sometimes these rumours were spread by the smugglers to increase the rates. The less risky routes were to Scandinavian countries and The Netherlands, as these countries had relatively generous asylum policies.

## Biographical vignette

Mahmood was a *dal lal* in the 1980s in New Delhi. He had come to India to do his master's degree in sociology at a university in New Delhi. I met him for the first time in late 1987. He, his wife, and their newborn child lived in a small apartment in New Friends Colony. He was one of the *dal lals* in New Delhi and a close friend of Nour's. The fare he offered me was reasonable, but he usually sent his clients via Bangkok, a route that entailed excessive risk. I did not want to travel further east any more.

Almost two decades later, on a July afternoon in 2008, I met Mahmood again. It was a rainy day and when I, wet from head to toe, jumped into his small framing store in downtown Toronto, he hugged me like an old friend. There was no trace of the young energetic Mahmood who talked intensely and was always headed somewhere. In front of me, in the framing store in Toronto, I saw a man who seemed aged and tired. With a few days' growth of beard, unkempt hair and a shabby shirt hanging over his pants, he seemed older than his age. I was in Toronto that summer as visiting scholar at the Centre for Refugee Studies, York University. Pour, my roommate in Hotel Shalimar, who was also now living in Toronto, had found Mahmood's phone number for me. I was unsure whether he would want to talk about his work and life in New Delhi. Contrary to my doubts, he did not mind talking about his past as a *dal lal*. 'I did not do it only for the money. Where would all those Iranians have gone if we did not help them?'

Since the framing business was not particularly successful, in the rear of the store he also took 'rapid-ready' passport photos. I stayed with him all afternoon until he closed. Between cups of herbal tea and stories of his clients, he took passport photos of people, Indians, Kenyans, Jamaicans, mainly from his neighbourhood. He jokingly said, 'Business as usual'.

He asked about those from that time in New Delhi with whom I was still in touch. He was eager to know what happened to the Iranian refugee community in New Delhi. He recalled the 'good' old days in New Delhi with nostalgia. Then, he was a well-known *dal lal*, a person Iranians needed for his advice and assistance. But now, in his small framing store, far from New Delhi, his only regular visitor was an old Kenyan man who lived next to his store. I asked him why he became a *dal lal*.

> It was not planned. My brother-in-law fled from Iran and came to India. He was in danger and wanted to be in a safe country, but did not have the money to hire a *dal lal*. So I thought if others can do it, why can't I? I sent him myself. You remember – it was easy then, in the early 1980s. After him I sent one more and then one more. I needed money. The Iranian state had blocked my stipend because of my political activities. I had no money and there were no jobs to take in India. So I started sending people to have a livelihood.

Mahmood said that the smuggling did not bring in a lot of money. For each person, he would pay USD 1000 for a ticket and between USD 200 and 400 for airport officers. He used cheap or second-grade passports to keep expenses low. In the end, around USD 500 would be left for him. 'Many of us, even your *dal lal*, Nour, worked like this. None of us got rich in this business. Many even went bankrupt'.

Human smuggling also meant financial risks for *dal lals* like Mahmood.

> If a client was arrested or deported, we [*dal lals*] would pay USD 200.00–300.00 to get him or her released. Sometimes the *dal lal* would send the client again without demanding extra money. This meant losses. Do you remember Karim? Once he sent ten people on the same flight to Europe. It was really foolish. They were of course discovered and were deported back to New Delhi. He went back with twenty thousand dollars. He paid a lot in bribes to get them out of jail and sent some of them once again. That became his end – he disappeared after that.

Mahmood said that he was cheated by several clients who did not pay him the rest of the fee after they arrived in the destination country. Like many other *dal lals*, Mahmood worked alone. He had no networks outside New Delhi. The only person he worked with was an officer who worked in the departure lounge at New Delhi airport: 'But I did not pay him every time I sent a person. Sometimes no one was paid. In cases when the passenger was self-assured and the passport was well forged, I pretended that the airport officer had been bribed so the passenger would feel safe.'

It was getting near dusk and he was going to close his store. He insisted on taking me home for dinner. Pour had told me that, after his wife divorced him a few years earlier, Mahmood lived alone in a small room near his store. So I thanked him, hugged him hard and expressed the wish to see him again. Outside the store and after he locked the door, he turned to me and said in a gloomy tone: 'I did not do it for money. If I had, my life would not be like this today'.

## The performance of border rituals

An 'illegal' journey is, after all, arbitrary. Sometimes the migrants end up in a particular country by sheer coincidence. Three months after my journey to Sweden, Hamid, another friend from Defence Colony, paid USD 2600 to Nour for Norway. Nour put him and an Afghan man on the same flight. The young Afghan man had never travelled by air before and was nervous. His hand was shaking when he gave his passport to the immigration officer, who apparently had not been bribed. The Afghan man was arrested at once. Hamid, who was a few metres behind him, saw the young man being removed by the police. The journey had become too risky so Hamid turned back. Nour could not send anyone for several months. His bribed contact person at the airport was removed. In the summer of 1988, Hamid paid a few hundred dollars extra and Nour sent him to Canada. If the hand of the Afghan man had not shaken, Hamid would now be living in Norway and not in Canada. One main difference between human smuggling and human trafficking is said to be 'control of one's movements', it means that the client can choose her or his destination. In my experience, however, the distinction is vague and incorrect.

Nour demanded half of the payment in advance to start the 'project'. We agreed that the rest would be paid when I reached my destination. A friend in Defence Colony would do that after receiving a call from me. Nour said that I should contact him regularly. The journey could not be planned too far in advance. Due to all the security factors involved, we could only know the day of departure one or two days in advance. The most important item for the travelling process was an appropriate passport. Some smugglers use a 'lookalike' strategy, which entails finding a passport whose former owner looks like the client to avoid altering the passport. New Delhi was a huge market for European passports. Many backpackers sold their passports when their money ran out. *Dal lals* bought passports from tourists in the railway station in New Delhi.

For a few hundred dollars, one could get a Danish, German, Spanish or Greek passport. Southern European passports were much in demand and therefore more expensive, due to the Mediterranean look of these nationals. An Iranian could pass more easily as Greek or Italian than as German. Another factor that determined the price of a passport was the amount of stamps inside it. More visa stamps and entry/exit stamps in a passport made it more bona fide and hence more expensive. Passports are the means a state uses to govern its population's movements (Torpey 2000). They link individuals to foreign policy and according to which travellers can be classified as safe or dangerous, desirable or undesirable (Salter 2004: 72). Passports determine our spatial limits or surplus rights of mobility. Thus, the passports of rich countries confer more mobility and therefore represent assets. The demand for forged passports of rich countries reflects the passport hierarchy existing in the black market.

However, Nour did not waste money on a real passport for me. He *made* one. It was a so-called 'second-grade' passport. 'Second-grade' passports were in fact photocopied passports. Using photocopied passports was a way to keep expenses low. They were also used when no good passports were available. The method of making a passport was primitive, using a photocopy machine, scissors and paste. Mine was a Greek passport. The first time I saw it I thought it was a joke. It was not even copied skilfully. The letterhead on some pages were crooked and some parts of the text at the top of the pages were missing. The cover was worse. It would not even fool the parking attendant at the airport, let alone an immigration officer. Nour said that the passport was not a big issue and that the immigration officer would be bribed to overlook it. Nour would also get the boarding card himself. I was unable to protest. I had already paid him half the agreed sum and the rate for Europe had increased by then to USD 2600.

In mid-February, Nour informed me that his *khat* to The Netherlands had been discovered by European police. He had decided to stop sending *mosafers* to The Netherlands for some time. I should wait a few months to see what would happen. Nour asked whether I wanted to go to Sweden instead. If so, I could be there in a week. 'Sweden?' I did not even know the geographical location of Sweden in Europe. 'Volvo?' said Nour. After 18 months living on borders, I did not really care where I ended up. Nour also said that Sweden still accepted Iranians. I believed him. During my time in New Delhi, I had rarely seen a deportee from Sweden. Sweden was 'a safe bet'. The 'illegal' journey is indeed a kind of gamble. Information, payment and networks are crucial and necessary components of an 'illegal' border crossing, but it is, after all, always a matter of chance.

On 27 February 1988, Nour handed me the passport and ticket and said that departure would be the next day. We would meet at the airport. I had a night to prepare my role as the Greek owner of the passport. My first name was Kostas and the surname, which I never learned by heart, was four or five centimetres long and impossible for me to pronounce. The whole night before departure, I tried to say and write *my* name by heart. As a symbol of the nation-state, the passport is a powerful document; it contains detailed information about the traveller, ranging from biometric data (identifying specific parts of the body) to place of birth, nationality and place of residence. A traveller must live up to her or his passport (Adey 2004:510) – we belong to our passports and not vice versa. Holding a Greek passport, I was supposed to live up to my Greek identity.

Since I could not count on my photocopied passport, I was depending greatly on my performance. Border crossing is, after all, a matter of performance. Borders are zones of cultural production, spaces of meaning-making and meaning-breaking (Donnan and Wilson 1999:64). Border crossing reinforces and challenges our social and political status. It has its own ritual – obtaining a passport, applying for a visa, passing security checks, and the performance of passing through specific places and spaces of border control and customs. Border crossing, being in 'borderland' (Hannerz 1997), a zone of betwixt and between, a predicament of liminality (Turner 1967 ), is, in an anthropological sense, a ritual. The border ritual reproduces the meaning and order of the state system. The border ritual is a secular and modern liturgy with its own rite of sacrifice.

Nour gave me some instructions for the border performance. The first rule was to stay cool and not to panic. If you are self-assured, you can cross any border even with the worst passport in your hand. But your body can betray you, and border guards can recognize the tell-tale signs at once. It is the body of the border crosser that displays the signs: furtive eyes, sweaty palms, nervous tension when answering questions (Donnan and Wilson 1999:131). Body performance is the central part of the ritual. The body should be disguised and trained to move. Those with Northern European passports should have the proper-coloured hair, eyebrows and even hair on their arms. 'Correct' dress was yet another part of the masquerade. Tony Saint, a former immigration officer at Heathrow airport, in his book *Refusal Shoes*, tells how a traveller's clothes might determine whether or not he or she gets an entry visa. Sometimes the 'wrong' pair of shoes was enough to cast suspicion on a traveller (Saint 2005). Except for Saman, who had a Saudi Arabian passport and was dressed 'properly' in a suit and tie, to act as a well-to-do businessman, the rest of us were to be back-packer types. Sometimes the smuggler sent one male and one female client as a couple. Their belongings were mixed and they were given instructions on how to perform to give the impression of being a married couple. The situation was even more complicated if a child was involved. It was difficult to induce a child to call a strange man 'daddy'. Language skills were also important, and those who could not speak English were sent with those who could.

To learn how to perform, I had spent many hours in Connaught Place and Tourist Camp, areas of New Delhi with high concentrations of tourists, to observe their bodily movements, gestures, clothes and bags. Sometimes I got into conversations with them just to learn more about them and their journeys. I wanted to know how and why they had come to India. I asked them about their backgrounds in their homelands and other matters.

Another source of inspiration for border performance was Hollywood. Amir, an old friend in both Hotel Shalimar and then Defence Colony, was inspired by *Midnight Express*. The protagonist of the film, who had packets of drugs taped to his body, felt profusely nervous going through immigration control. Before going through, the protagonist went to the washroom and kept taking very short, rapid breaths for several minutes to bring his breathing under control. The night before his departure to The Netherlands, Amir talked a lot about this specific scene and how he would imitate the protagonist. Similarly, Yaghmaian, in describing the journeys of 'illegal' immigrants in Europe, observes how they learn border crossing methods from movies (Yaghmaian 2005:266). It is a subversive tactic, in de Certeau's (1984) words, used by the 'illegal' migrants, who attempt to catch the elusive moment when it is possible to realize individual preferences, to challenge power by continually manipulating events in the system in order to subvert the dominant border regime.

According to my passport, I was a young Greek tourist in India, so I had to act like one. Amir gave me his red T-shirt and Hoshang his sneakers. With a second-hand backpack, I looked a little more like a tourist. I met Nour in the departure lounge at the airport. He gave me the boarding cards and detailed instruction as to what I should do. He said that his contact person, an immigration officer, would take care of the rest. Finally, he showed me where to go and wished me good luck. I went to the first counter from the left. I do not remember how long I stood there in front of the officer and stared at his fingers browsing through my photocopied passport. Was there really a 'contact' or had Nour just lied? I was anxious and wanted to run, but where to? There was no going back. The fear and anguish I felt in front of the immigration officer that day cannot be put in words. But Nour had done an excellent job. My trip went smoothly all the way to Arlanda airport in Stockholm via London with that strange photocopied passport.

Heathrow was my transit airport. The flight was arranged in such a way that I was several hours in transit, making it more difficult for the Swedish police to trace my flight and country of departure. Needless to say, I was not to carry any identification other than my Greek passport. As such, I had left letters, photos and my Iranian ID cards behind, to be sent to me when I reached Sweden. I had searched my pockets and belongings thoroughly. Anything – such as an Indian coin or even a stamp – could reveal my route. To reduce the risk of deportation, it was important not to let the police in the country of destination know what flight and route I had taken. Somewhere between London and Stockholm, following Nour's instructions, I tore up the passport, boarding pass and ticket and flushed them down the toilet. Nour told me that, to make it difficult to trace me back to India, I should spend a few hours waiting in Arlanda airport before going to the police.

For 'illegal' travellers, there are no better places than transit halls: rootless places without local identity, where everybody is a stranger, a traveller. 'Illegal' travellers find themselves at *home* in transit halls, while it is the opposite to home for all others. A transit hall is a nonplace, disconnected from local history, identity and culture (Augé 1995). Devoid of social interaction, culture and history, a non-place is a functional space for the 'juxtaposition of solitudes'. Everybody arrives at the transit hall to leave, but for more and more travellers without documents, caught between borders, transit halls have become places for longer stays.

Undocumented travellers can be found in most large airports. Some stay briefly, others longer, trapped in the cracks between nation-states. They embody borders. One of them was Zahra Kamalfar, an Iranian woman with her two children, 18 and 10 years old, who spent 11 months in Sheremetyevo Airport, Moscow, until Canada offered them refugee status in March 2007. However, the best-known transit hall resident is undoubtedly Mehran Karimi, known also as Sir Alfred. He lived 18 years, between August 1988 and July 2006, in Terminal 1 at Charles de Gaulle Airport, Paris. He received refugee status in 1980 in Belgium. In 1986, on his way to England, his bag was stolen at Charles de Gaulle Airport. Without documents, he was deported back from Heathrow to Charles de Gaulle Airport. The Belgian authorities refused to send him his refugee documents and claimed that he had to present himself in person in Belgium so they could identify him. According to Belgian law, a refugee who leaves the country is not welcome back. In a Kafkaesque situation, Mehran Karimi was trapped in a corner of the Terminal 1, near McDonald's. A Hollywood adaption of his life for screen was made by Steven Spielberg in 2004 entitled *The Terminal*, in which the stateless border transgressor (Tom Hanks) in the end of the film is saved (welcomed in the US) by an employee of the airport (Catherine Zeta-Jones) who falls in love with him. The real Mehran Karimi has been less lucky than Tom Hanks. I visited him at Charles de Gaulle Airport in June 2004 and had a short conversation over a cup of coffee. He was sick, and two years later he was moved to a hospital and later to a charity reception centre (see his autobiography, Mehran and Donkin 2004).

Airports are settings for late-capitalist human mobility, juxtaposing consumption (transit terminals resemble shopping malls), class division (VIP lounges and sections, first-class seats), and racialized 'surveillant sorting' (Adey 2004) that distinguishes undesirable from desirable mobilities.

At Arlanda airport, two policemen waited at the gate and picked out 'asylum seeker-looking' passengers. My masquerade and 'performance' did not work in Sweden. Along with a few other people who looked like asylum seekers, we were taken to the police station at the airport, albeit still in the transit area. We waited in a corridor outside a door, just before entering the luggage area. There were only a few chairs. Some of us sat on the floor and others stood along the walls while regular passengers passed by. Border experiences are shaped by class and gender (Buijs 1993) and by one's position in the hierarchy of nations or ethnicities (Löfgren 1999).

Border crossing can be experienced in terms of honour and shame (cf. Kumar 2000). A legal journey is regarded as an honourable act in the spirit of globalism and cosmopolitanism. The legal traveller crosses the border gloriously and, in so doing, enhances his or her social status, whereas the border transgressor is antithetical, being seen as shamed and anti-ethical (they are called 'illegal' and depicted as unprivileged, poor and useless victims). We live in an era of 'world apartheid', where borders differentiate individuals. While, for some, the border confers a 'surplus of rights'; for others it is a 'colour bar' (Balibar 2002:78–84). Freedom of mobility for some is only possible through the organized exclusion of others (Cresswell 2006:233). Airport functions include screening and filtering out threats to the nation using the technique of profiling. Profiling is intended to identify potential threats, murderers, terrorists or travellers without passports. The sorting mechanism mirrors the broader global order of bordering, whereby people are sorted into 'kinetic elites and kinetic underclasses' (Adey 2006). Access or lack of access to global mobility has become a new form of social stratification in a globalizing world. It has resulted in the extraterritoriality of the new global elites and the forced territoriality of the rest (Bauman 1998). Consequently, an immobile global underclass has emerged.

For the first time since I crossed the Iran–Afghanstan border, my first border, I was struck by the shame of my migrant illegality. Nowhere else had I experienced the border so tangibly, powerfully and distressingly. Shame is part of the punishment for transgressing nation-state sovereignty. Many of my friends told me later how humiliated they felt saying 'I am a refugee' when they arrived at the destination country. The worst was that I internalized the shame and for many years lied about my route to Sweden. I pretended to be a quota refugee, one of the thousands of conventional refugees to whom the Swedish government annually offers resettlement in Sweden. Shame is the experience of being exposed to the disapproving gaze of others. There is a risk that the 'illegal' migrant, subjected to a gaze and treatment that divest him or her of humanity, will internalize the shame – as I did – and understand the lack of travel documents and documentation as personal deficiencies and inadequacies. The importance and centrality of shame in the experience of migration is still unexplored.

After waiting for a long time in the corridor I was called inside a room. The police searched me and asked me about my flight and transit country. Following Nour's instructions, I answered that I was Iranian and had come via Dubai. Nour believed that Europeans did not deport Iranians to Dubai, where 'illegal' migrants are brutally punished before being sent back to their countries of origin. The police did not believe me and said that I had come from Istanbul. My denial did not help and he said that I would be sent to Istanbul. I was put in the detention centre at Arlanda airport for two days.

I had no money left in New Delhi and my contract with Nour lacked a guarantee. This meant that, in case of deportation, he would not pay to take me out of detention, let alone send me on my way again. The thought of being sent to Istanbul, notorious for treating border transgressors brutally and a city where I knew no one then, was frightening. The cell was small and cold. I was given only sheets made of tissue material, to prevent suicide attempts. The journey I had begun one and half years earlier seemed lengthy, but I had indeed moved only from one border prison to another. Through a small window opening on the runways, I watched countless landings and departures of international airlines transporting those with 'surplus' mobility rights while I was fixed in immobility.

A police officer interviewed me at length on the second day. It was a cold February day and the window was half open. I was freezing in the light jacket I had worn from hot New Delhi. When I mentioned this to the police officer, in the hope that he would close the window, he said, 'You refugees always overdramatize'. What, I thought then, would he say if I told him the story of Hotel Shalimar and its guests and their stories of death, rape, suicide and pain?

Lacking any documents or evidence that could indicate that I had come from Istanbul made my deportation to Turkey impossible. The Turkish border authorities would send me immediately back to Sweden. On the third day, I was handed over to the Migration Board.

# 4
## The Invisible Border

### The Arctic camp

My first residence in Sweden after being released from detention was a refugee camp in Kiruna, the northernmost city in Sweden, 145 kilometres north of the Arctic Circle. Through the window of the airplane, as far as our sight reached, there was only snow and woodland. No immigrant communities existed in that little Arctic town. With our dark black hair or skin, we stuck out everywhere we went. People looked at us as if we were space aliens.

One aspect of migrant illegality is that one's life is unsettled, unpredictable and erratic. Migrant illegality means abrupt and dramatic interruptions in one's life, interruptions such as detention, deportation or simply sudden opportunities to move. Migrants disappear without a trace. I lost contact with many of my co-travellers from Cantt Station and Defence Colony, and I do not know what happened to them. However, I have followed some in their trajectory wanderings (see Appendix). We use all kinds of communication, ranging from personal networks – extending from Los Angeles via London to Tehran – to Facebook to find old co-travellers. Like war veterans, a shared trauma, a collective woe, binds us together. When we meet, our talk is almost entirely about Cantt Station, Defence Colony and shared friends who passed through these places. We have lost something over there.

Once again, my life was lived with refugees and immigrants from all corners of the poor world, with Asians, Africans and Latin Americans. We all had one thing in common, our homelessness and wondering what the hell we were doing in a city covered with frost and darkness. Daylight was limited to a few hours per day. To make things cosier, the camp was attacked by an anti-immigrant mob one week after my arrival. Despite all the differences (not least in terms of economic resources) between my Arctic camp and refugee camps in poor countries in Asia and Africa, the logic of the camp, however, was the same: to place undesired people outside the society. The camp meant both expelling and excepting refugees.

Camps are for refugees – those *exceptions* to the nation-state system who have violated the norm and are unfeasible to be integrated into the ordinary law. Refugee camps are the most advanced form of the global treatment of stigmatized identities and undesirable groups (Agier 2008:61). They treat refugees like lepers in the Middle Ages, who were kept outside city walls. The French anthropologist Michel Agier has observed that refugee camps are not only spatially but temporally outside the commonplace and outside the ordinary and predictable world (Agier 2008:40). Camps are spaces but not places. Refugee camps, even those that have existed for several decades and house a constant population of tens of thousands, like small towns, do not appear on the maps of countries (Agier 2008:44). Camps occupy space but are not recognized as official places. Their inhabitants live, give birth and die there for generations but are not recognized as a community. Camps are unnamable, indefinable.

Regarded as having penetrated the 'purity' of the nation, refugees are seen as constituting a 'danger' (Douglas 1966). To protect the wellbeing of society, these individuals are placed under surveillance, located outside the sphere of ordinary social life. By regulating, managing and limiting refugee mobility, camps function to protect the virtue of the nation. In the case of Nazi camps, the juridical foundation of internment was *Schuzhaft* (literally: protective custody). Metaphorically, the Swedish word *förvar* (detention centre) is often confused with *försvar* (defense) (Khosravi 2009a). The camp is not a historical relic of the past, but is 'the hidden matrix and *nomos* of the political space in which we still live' (Agamben 2000:36). Refugee camps constitute the most significant characteristic of the modern nation-state. One significant feature of all refugee camps, no matter where they are located, is that they impose 'refugeeness', not as a juridical category but rather as a mode of being, an identity, on individuals. As Malkki puts it: 'refugeeness is a matter of becoming' (1997:228).

Through a pathologizing bureaucracy, camps produce refugees, or rather refugeeness. As a war refugee, I was not seen as a 'normal' and 'healthy' individual. Apart from the medical examinations of my body, I was treated, according to the most positive interpretation, as a child who did not know what was good or bad for him. The clientization of the refugee began as soon as she or he entered the camp. In the Arctic camp, I was educated to become a 'victim'. Neither lashes on my back, time in prison nor a year of statelessness could take from me my dignity as the Arctic camp did. Until then, I might have lacked documents and a state, yet I was full of life, will and courage. All that I lost in the process of 'becoming a refugee'. As a Rwandan man in a refugee camp put it, 'they educate us to be refugees' (Malkki 1995a:222).

I, who had crossed so many borders and lived in dangerous places, shared rooms with prostitutes and a cell with a murderer and drug smugglers, had become afraid to take the bus to the city centre, in one of the safest countries in the world. This deeply embodied fear stayed with me for a long time. Even today, though to a much lesser extent, I suffer from agoraphobia – a fear of being among others, of being seen. In that period of my life, I wrote a couple of amateurish short stories, which I never submitted for publication. One was about a young black man who always wore dark sunglasses, day and night, indoors and outdoors. He was protecting himself from the collective judgmental gaze. He could see without being seen. The other was about a young man who realized that he simply did not exist for others, when one day in the subway he talked to people and no one heard him and one woman simply walked right through him to get on the train.

The victim role followed me for a long time beyond the walls of the refugee camp. I first realized how deeply the role had become internalized many years later in the mid-1990s during a course on anthropological methodology when I was interviewed by a classmate as part of the course's practical work. For refugees, interviews are associated with the asylum process, meetings with refugee camp authorities or encounters with border police. My classmate, a young Swedish woman, focused the interview on my life. In the middle of the interview, I saw her eyes were getting wet and then suddenly tears were running down her chin. Obviously, I was telling her exactly what I was supposed to say as a refugee in an interview. I had left no space for enjoyment, agency, self-representation or individual background. In that interview, as I had been 'educated', my self-represented victim role appeared, stripped of the specificity of culture, place and history (Malkki 1995a).

Years later, I reluctantly became a link between my informants, failed asylum seekers, and the Swedish media. Refugees are not only 'helpless', they are also 'speechless' and need someone to speak for them, for example, journalists, researchers, politicians and activists (Malkki 1997:236). It was my informants who asked me to help them into the public sphere. These failed asylum seekers believed that publicity would give them a second chance. I always followed my informants and was the interpreter. My informants knew well what was expected of them. Noting how asylum seekers are discursively constituted as 'non-agents', they strategically appropriated that discourse in their own self-presentation through performing 'victimcy' (Utas 2005:409). Utas demonstrates that victimcy is a form of self-representation deployed by Liberian refugees in their 'social navigation' of displacement. Several of my informants used the interviews with journalists as a chance to gain advantage through performing victimcy and refugeeness. By exaggerating and overplaying their subjugation, they were performing the role ascribed to them. They had been educated to perform in such a way.

My informants were aware that displaying any kind of agency would cast the authenticity of their refugeeness into doubt. Once one informant, a young Kurdish woman in her early twenties whose asylum application had been rejected, had an appointment with her lawyer before going to the Migration Board. I followed her to a café where she was supposed to meet her lawyer. When the lawyer came, she started by commenting on the young woman's looks and dress. The lawyer, also a woman, told my informant to wipe off her makeup and change from her miniskirt into jeans, because in her current condition 'she did not look like a refugee'.

Refugeeness entails living up to expectations of what a refugee is. Malkki (1995a:9) has indicated that there is a 'tendency to universalize "the refugee" as a special "kind" of person, not only in the textual representation, but also in their photographic representation'.

The stereotype of 'the refugee' and what she or he 'looks like' is formed by visual representations in the form of abundant images in the press, on TV and recently even in coffee-table books (see, for example, Szörényi 2006). Wright believes that such images of refugees are primarily rooted in Christian religious iconography, which has a long tradition of portraying forced migration; witness such themes as 'the expulsion from the Garden of Eden' and 'the flight into Egypt' (Wright 2000). Furthermore, refugeeness and asylum are linked to old biblical traditions such as 'cities of refuge' and 'sanctuary'. Wright (2000) demonstrates that there are 'striking similarities in content and style' between Christian iconography and the current visual representation of refugees. Refugees are portrayed as embodied eternal human suffering.

Some images of refugees have become an allegory of refugeeness. The best-known example is the picture of the 'Afghan Girl', Sharbat Gula, taken in a refugee camp in Pakistan. Her innocent, childish and beautiful face, with green eyes staring into the camera, appeared on the cover of *National Geographic* in June 1985. The 'Afghan Girl' image has appeared extensively in newspapers, magazines, handbooks, brochures and on TV. The visual representation of refugees often reduces them to bearers of the 'message', to signifiers of the 'real world' for viewers in rich parts of the world (Szörényi 2006).

In other words, pain and suffering have become the hallmarks of refugeeness. The term 'refugee' generally signifies deprived and underprivileged people. A 'real' refugee is thus supposed to be a 'profound', 'poor', 'traumatized', 'serious' and of course 'sad' person. I was once told by a refugee case worker in Sweden that Iranians could not be 'real' refugees. To my 'Why?' she answered, 'You see, they are well-dressed and go to discos'. Thus, a happy, well-dressed, good-looking refugee is a contradiction. Refugees have to perform 'refugeeness'. Similarly, the authenticity of smuggled asylum seekers' cases may be called into question because they have paid 'a lot of money to the smuggler'.

The feeling of estrangement and alienation, not only from Swedish society but, in an existential sense, from the world in general, was intensified in the frozen refugee camp north of the Arctic Circle. By then, even the atrocious Hotel Shalimar seemed a remote haven. All these symptoms are woes of exile, of being out of place, of having no place. According to an old Afghan legend, the soul leaves the body when one dreams. If one wakes up before one's soul has returned to the body, one enters an eternal nightmare (*kabous*), an outlandish predicament. For me this is what exile is about: my soul did not return in time. Exile is when you live in one place and dream in another. Exile is a dream of going back home. In exile, one is possessed by longing, no matter where the exile takes place. The whole world becomes a prison. Neither Calypso's beauty and passionate love nor a pleasant life on her island could relieve Odysseus's longing for Ithaca. A life in exile is like being condemned to purgatory, a state between life and death, a limbo between here and there. Like many others in exile, I have an ambivalent relationship with space and time. My body is physically here and now while my heart is there and then. The spatial dimension of exilic life is excluding, vicious and wounding. In allocating the social spaces, the exiles are not counted.

Exile can therefore be felt bodily. I feel it in my agoraphobia. In exile, not even time follows its normal rhythm. In exile, the past exists side by side with the present. Exilic life is the constant presence of the absent. I am in the subway and waiting for the train, ordering a coffee in a coffee shop, paying money in a grocery store, eating lunch with my colleagues on campus, listening to a lecturer, writing a word on the blackboard for my students, and then abruptly images of our houses, hazelnut trees, vineyard, a breeze moving through the tree-tops outside my room in our Bakhtiari house, or mountains appear before my eyes. Unexpected and unintentional the images come, one by one, like a slide show. The images are detailed and real, but disappear as swiftly as they appear. They are an interruption in the rhythm of the present, an intermezzo. In exile, one does not stand on firm ground. Exile is a condition of transience. Since crossing the border to Afghanstan, everything has been provisional, transitory. Exile is only parenthetic to life, though it lasts and lasts, though I know return is only a myth, a never-to-be-realized dream, though I know there is no home to go back to. Even though the house is there, the home is gone. I am not the same person, either. When Odysseus returned to Ithaca, no one recognized him, not even his beloved Penelope. However, the dream keeps me hoping. It liberates me from the unbearable burden of alienhood.

After six months I was granted asylum on humanitarian grounds. I thought I had experienced all the possible kinds of borders.

I assumed that there would be no more borders ahead to be crossed. However, I had a new kind of border to tackle.

## Invisible borders

After crossing many physical, national borders, I found myself facing other kinds of borders in Sweden, those in the minds of people. When I thought the journey had been completed and the destination reached, I still found myself standing before invisible borders, more difficult or impossible to cross. These borders were intangible and elusive, yet powerful and deep rooted. I have survived crossing many borders between nation-states in dangerous places, surviving bandits, corrupt border guards, statelessness and lack of status, but these invisible borders have, since my arrival in Sweden more than two decades ago, pushed me into a corner.

The invisible borders are as intractable as the visible ones, and the wounds they inflict no less real. The bleeding caused by crossing these borders might be less acute than those inflicted by a physical border, but it lasts longer. On the night of crossing the border into Afghanstan, scared and tired of the endless hiking, I complainingly asked Homayoun when we would reach the border. He would reassuringly answer, 'after the next peak'. Yet there was always another peak to be passed after the next one. We did reach the border. An invisible border, however, is unreachable. You think you can see it: you touch it, or rather it touches you. But just when you assume you can grab hold of it, it fades away. This experience resembles Sisyphus' plight. In Greek mythology Sisyphus was sentenced by the gods to roll a huge rock up a hill, but just before he could reach the top, the rock would always roll back down, forcing him to begin again. The border gaze does not permit a sense of belonging to the new country to emerge. One's will and ability to join in withers. For many, it becomes a choice between a Sisyphusian attempt to cross the border and recognizing the impenetrability of the wall, the border, thereby abandoning the idea of becoming part of the new society. The border gaze does not operate through a simple function of exclusion. It situates immigrants on the 'threshold', between inside and outside. They are given no chance to develop a sense of belonging but are nonetheless expected to participate. They have not been thrown out, but neither are they considered participants or part of the context. Undesirable immigrants are included without being members. 'The exception is that which cannot be included in the whole of which it is a member and cannot be a member of the whole in which it is always already included' (Agamben 1998:25).

The invisible border keeps immigrants strangers for generations. The Sisyphusian plight of integration extends even to the next generation. The border exposes me to a gaze that does not *see* me as an individual but *reads* me as a type. The visual field is not neutral. The gaze is a hierarchically interwoven complex of gender, racial and class factors. In his theory of *otherness*, Sartre explores the power of gaze both in his most famous play *No Exit* (1989 [1944]) and in *Being and Nothingness* (1956:252–261). In *No Exit*, three people find themselves in hell, which is in fact a living room. Instead of physical torture, each character is exposed to the process of objectification by being looked at. Each person attempts to make the two others into his/her objects, and thereby make himself/herself the subject. The subject (the one who looks) remakes the object (the one who is looked at) and denies his or her individuality outside the subject's mind. Constantly being the target of the 'devouring' and judging gaze of each other, one character says, 'Hell is other people'. In his classic *Black Skin, White Masks* (1994 [1952]), Frantz Fanon set Sartre's thesis on othering in a colonial context, and demonstrated how the colonial gaze 'objectifies' and 'fixes' the black man and woman both racially and sexually.

Rainer Werner Fassbinder in his magnificent film *Angst essen Seele auf* (Ali: Fear Eats the Soul) impressively illustrates the power of the border gaze. Depicting the relationship between a young African man and a late-middle-aged German woman, Fassbinder tells us that, for the couple, there is no way out of the collective gaze that forces them into isolation and failure. In one scene, Ali and his beloved are sitting in an outdoor café. They are the only guests. The camera turns and shows a bunch of café staff standing in a line and staring at them. The couple at first try to ignore them, but their gaze is insistent and penetrating. The border gaze is also a central theme in Roman Polanski's *The Tenant*. An omnipresent border gaze drives a young Polish refugee man in Paris to distorted self-perception, madness and finally a tragic suicide attempt.

The gaze is not an innocent act of seeing, but an episteme determining who/what is visible and invisible. One of the most notorious aspects of the mode of seeing is racial. Ralph Ellison, in his classic *Invisible Man* (first published in 1952), is perhaps the first who brought to light the racial production of the visual. It is a story of an African-American man's experience of being ignored and refused acknowledgement in a racist America. But while he is effectively invisible, society 'observes' his every move. He is, however, visible only – to borrow Rushdie's words from *Satanic Verses* – in others' fantasies. 'When they approach me they see only my surroundings, themselves, or figments of their imagination – indeed, everything and anything except me' (Ellison 1987 [1952]:7). In other words, this xenophobic gaze is not only seeing but also reading (Butler 1993:16). The (in)visibility of African-Americans has played a crucial role in constructing the white American identity (see Williams 1991).

The border gaze is not only racialized but also gendered. Moreover, the border reproduces the dominant gender stereotype. While women are targeted by the border in relation to their sexuality, men are targeted in relation to their religion and ethnicity. In the case of Muslim men, the gender and racial aspects of the border intersect, making Muslim men the main targets of the current border regime. Moral panic emerged after 11 September 2001, and, in connection with the 'War on Terror', it pursues Muslims and particularly Muslim men. The 'War on Terror' has been conflated with border regimes and thereby restricts, controls and defines the movement and mobility of men of Muslim belief (De Genova 2007). Iconic male Muslim figures, such as Bin Ladin, Saddam Hussein or the 9/11 hijackers, have come to personify the antithesis of 'civilized' Western values and norms. The gendered xenophobic border gaze defines, fixes and excludes Muslim men (Hunt and Rygiel 2006; Ewing 2008; Khosravi 2009b).

The 'primitive masculinity' ascribed to Muslim men is a way to represent them, not only as a danger to Muslim women but also as a force that violates Swedish norms and values. Muslim men are stereotyped as more likely to violate Western norms and values than are Muslim women. Their 'primitive masculinity' is seen as inferior to the 'civilized' masculinities of Western men (see Khosravi 2009b). Indeed, the Muslim man is also seen as endangering the passive Muslim woman, who is a victim needing to be saved. Such stereotyping may explain why Switzerland allows five times more female than male Muslim asylum seekers to remain for humanitarian reasons (Holzer, Schneider and Widmer 2000, cited in Noll and Aleksandra 2006). Accordingly, more male than female Muslim asylum seekers are subjected to removal (Khosravi 2009a). The sex-discriminative feature of the border regime is revealed by the case of 'unaccompanied male asylum seekers' from Afghanstan. In May 2007, a Swedish Migration Board guiding decision declared that 'Afghan unaccompanied men will forcibly be deported in view of the fact that they have proper preconditions for being re-integrated'. There are similar attempts to justify the removal of 'unaccompanied male asylum seekers' from Somalia and Iraq. Muslim men are also seen as a danger to Western norms and values. The discourse used against Muslim men's 'primitive masculinity' was explicitly demonstrated by the newspaper clipping attached to a map of Sweden in the office of the chief of the division for immigration at the National Police Board. The clipping read: 'His view of women has no place in Sweden [*Hans kvinno syn hör inte till Sverige*]'. When I asked the division chief about the clipping, he explained that 'a lot of those [male asylum seekers] coming here do not share our values'. The intersection and interaction between ethnicity and gender and 'the ways in which each defines and depends on the other for its meaning and power' makes for what Nagel calls 'ethnosexual frontiers'. Just as nation-states expose 'illegal' travellers to necropolitics, the border gaze, through its xenophobic mode of seeing, targets and imperils the lives of undesirable immigrants. 'Border gaze', for those targeted by it, is more than an abstract theoretical concept; it is a highly tangible part of everyday life. It is forceful and sometimes formidable and deadly. On 21 October 1991, less than three years after my arrival in Sweden, I was shot in the face by a racist.

## Hos(ti)pitality

I had just moved to Stockholm, where I had started taking courses in Social Anthropology at Stockholm University. On that October night, I left the sports hall on the university campus at 10 pm. It was dark and cold. I headed to my room in the student residence, a few hundred metres away from the sports hall. There was a piece of woodland to the right of the footpath, part of a larger national park on the northern part of the campus. There was no-one else around. No more than 100 metres away from the sports hall I heard a sound, something like rustling leaves, coming from inside the woodland.

I looked in that direction but could see nothing. The moment I turned back, I was hit in the face. I heard nothing, but felt something like a big stone being smashed on my head. After a while, I found myself thrown on the ground, half unconscious, my body lying on the freezing asphalt and my face in a little pool of blood. I was afraid that more attacks would come, so I tried to protect my head with my arms. I heard some people standing around me. They looked at me but did not touch me, abandoning me in my blood. That they pretended not to see what they saw, looked but did not see, heard but did not listen, reacted with indifference and lack of curiosity to another's suffering, frightens me more than the possibility of being shot again. I later learned that a young Chinese guest student had run to ask for help. In hospital, I was told that I had been shot. A 0.22-calibre bullet had bored through my cheek on the right side of my face, had hit my teeth and split inside my mouth. Hearing that shocked and frightened me. Being shot in the face meant no chance of survival for me. I did not want to die like that, alone, anonymous, in a hospital so far away from the Bakhtiari and Hotel Shalimar and, worst of all, not knowing why I had been shot. For what crime? By whom? I did not want to die 'like a dog' – as Josef K. describes his own death in the last passage in *The Trial* (1999 [1925]). Two men take him to a quarry to be executed. He does not know for what crime he will be killed. He looks around to find a familiar face, help or at least compassion, in vain.

When the hospital staff realized that I had been shot, the doctors and nurses leapt into action around me. More staff came in. Several tubes and wires were attached to my body. The nurse, who was desperately trying to stop the bleeding, noticed that I was looking at the blood running down along my neck to my right arm, dropping from my fingers to the floor. To comfort me, she said something like 'What nice blood!' (*vilket bra blod*). It could not have been more ironic! She probably did not know by then, but I was sure that someone had just tried to kill me because of that very blood.

Since removing the remaining bullet fragments would have severely damaged my cheek, the doctors decided to leave them in my cheekbone. Bullet fragments are still lodged deep in my bones – souvenirs of the border gaze. Moreover, the bullet had also shattered sensory nerves on the right side of my chin, so I have forever lost the sense of feeling under my lower lip. My life's irony is that I had left my home and had come all the way to Sweden to escape guns and bullets. I never told my family about this. How could I?

The first police officers I met in hospital had clear judgments about me and the incident. They asked questions about 'the Iranian mafia' in Stockholm, whether I had anything to do with them, whether I had any enemies, or whether I was in political dispute with the Iranian state. Fortunately, the morphine saved me from both the unbearable pain and the police officers' agonizing questions.

The next day, a police inspector came to ask more questions. When he found out that I was unable to talk, he delivered a long speech on how troublesome Iranian immigrants were. He mentioned an incident in 1986 when Iranian opposition groups clashed with pro-Iranian state groups in central Stockholm and how it disturbed the peace of the city. I wanted to tell him that in 1986 I was still in Iran, unaware of his city, and that in my wildest fantasies could not have imagined ending up there.

I did not realize why he was telling me these things until years later, when I read an article by Judith Butler (1993) on Rodney King, an African-American man brutally beaten by Los Angeles police on 3 March 1991. He was first hit with a high-voltage Taser and then with metal batons. Around 20 policemen were present. The scene was recorded on videotape by a witness. Although racist brutality was undeniable, the lawyers of the police nevertheless used the video in court in an attempt to justify the policemen's brutality. In their interpretation of the video, the black body of Rodney King, being kicked on the ground, was the source of danger and the policemen's use of violence was justifiable 'self-defence'. By reproducing the 'circuit of paranoia' (Butler 1993), the *negrophobic* mode of seeing remade the black body of Rodney King into 'danger' threatening the 'purity' of the white policemen. 'The visual field is not neutral to the question of race; it is itself a racial formation, an episteme, hegemonic and forceful' (Butler 1993:17). The victim was turned into the offender. So it was in my case as well. The Swedish police inspector, by racializing me and identifying me as a source of danger, was obliquely saying, 'Shahram, you deserved it'.

I was still in hospital when another non-European immigrant was shot in Stockholm, and soon after him, another one and then one more. It soon turned out to be a case of a serial murderer who targeted immigrants. Since he used a rifle equipped with a laser sight, he was nicknamed the 'Laser Man' (*Lasermannen*). Between August 1991 and February 1992, he killed one and injured 10 seriously; I was the second target. He was arrested in June 1992. His name was Johan Wolfgang Alexander Ausonius. He was born in 1953 to a Swiss father and a German mother, both immigrants to Sweden. Throughout his childhood, he was bullied because of his black hair and non-Swedish name. As an adult, he dyed his hair blond and used Swedish names to pass as a Swede. His hatred of his black hair and his immigrant background turned into a hatred of non-European immigrants. The racist acts of the Laser Man were not independent of the larger political context. The Laser Man was thus a product of the harsh anti-immigrant political climate of early-1990s Sweden. Not surprisingly, John Ausonius became the Laser Man the same year *Nydemokrati*, the most anti-immigrant party of the time, entered parliament (see Tamas 2003). The other victims were not as fortunate as I was, as all of them were left more or less paralysed, though Jimmy, a young Iranian man, was the only one who was killed. The Laser Man was sentenced to life imprisonment.

More than ten years after he shot me, I received a letter from the Laser Man. He wrote that 'you should not take it personally' and that what he did was a critique of Swedish immigration policy. He wrote that he had no intention of killing or injuring anybody. He obviously wrote the letter in a bid for reduced prison time. Migrants pay the price of rebordering and debordering policies: they are sacrificed in the ritual of renegotiating the borders.

Did I take it personally? Being shot was obviously a personal and private experience for the simple reason that the very rationale for my being shot was my black hair. Nevertheless, the attack was linked to a larger political predicament where the private and public are indistinguishable. The intersection of the private and public has had formidable consequences for millions of people throughout the last century. Jews, Romani, homosexuals and the disabled were sent to the concentration camps by the Third Reich due to their very private and personal characteristics, namely their belief, 'blood', sexuality and bodily features. War rape in all conflicts, from the Balkans to the Congo, is another example of how the private body, sexuality and gender, conflated with 'blood', are interwoven with the macro-politics of warfare. Public and private events, political life and biological life – all have become indistinguishable (Agamben 2000:121). The intersection of private/biological life and public/political life as the origin of modern brutality is perhaps best manifested in Franz Kafka's *The Trial*, where the courtroom in which Josef K. is tried is next to the bedroom. This can explain why the Laser Man conflated the colour of my hair with public issues, such as migration policy and Swedish nationhood.

I sat in the victim's chair in court, before the law and before a long row of journalists who would later broadcast my name and my story all over the country, a large public affair caused because of the colour of my hair. My private body had become an issue in the public arena, as in Iran, when the cleric condemned me to flogging for a bottle of wine. For the cleric, the judge, my sin (a private personal deed) became synonymous with crime (public offence). Banality is always a crucial feature of political brutality. I have demonstrated elsewhere how 'trivial' things such as dancing, kissing, a *Playboy* magazine, a receiver for satellite TV channels, a pair of Nike sneakers or a bottle of home-made vodka could become part of the national political agenda in Iran (Khosravi 2008). Slavenka Drakulić, in her impressive description of everyday life in societies under communist regimes in Eastern Europe, describes similar patterns. Trivial acts such as eating pizza, wearing a fur coat or even using make-up were perceived as 'bourgeois manners'. 'A nicely dressed woman was subject to suspicion, sometimes even investigation' (Drakulić 1987:23). Brutality flourishes where the private and public are indistinguishable. In court, only a few metres from me, I faced for the first time the man who fired his gun at me just because he wanted 'to express his criticism of Swedish migration politics'. His hateful gaze was no less personal than it was public.

My name, my body and my history became topics in the public sphere, including the mass media and popular culture. Since the late 1990s, several books, both fiction (for example, Khemiri 2006) and non-fiction (for example, Tamas 2003), several TV documentaries and a TV series, not to mention innumerable reportage about the Laser Man and his victims have been published, produced and broadcast. The mode of representation of me and my story has been no less brutal than the act of shooting itself. Through the project of transforming my private self into a public subject, I have been renamed, re-shaped and re-defined. I will cite a few examples. A few weeks after the incident, I was interviewed by *Aftonbladet*, one of Sweden's main tabloids. For more than half an hour, I told my story to the journalist who recorded my voice and carefully took notes. I told him about the racism and how I was treated by the police. Two days later, my photo was on the front page of the newspaper (7 November 1991). But inside the newspaper, there were no words of mine. What I read in the newspaper was all fabricated by the journalist. To make it even worse, I was renamed 'Ali'. Under the photo it read: 'Ali thanks God he survived.' I was called Ali (a name with more Islamic connotations than Shahram) and was presented as a religious person.

Similarly, in the TV series *Lasermannen*, I was depicted wearing a beard (perhaps intended to resemble a member of the Taliban rather than a secular student of anthropology). At an early stage of producing the TV series, a woman from the production company called me to ask if they could use my name in the film. I did not give my permission, but she said that, in any case, they had the legal right to use my name. Swedish freedom of information legislation (*offentlighetsprincipen*) gives anyone right to access public records. I had no power over my name or story any more. It often happens that in a public speech or a lecture on a completely different subject, I am asked to say something about my experiences as a victim of the Laser Man. It is normally impossible and sometimes useless for me to attempt to keep the private distinct from the public.

The Laser Man, in his letter from prison, asked me not to take his bullet in my face personally, and I have to admit that I had not taken it personally. Everything, from being shot to the police, the legal process and the media, was surreal. From the outset, it was as if I was experiencing all the violence from the outside, as if it was someone else who had been shot. When I had been shot and was lying in my blood, an image appeared in my head of a young black man on his knees, surrounded by several white men with baseball bats in their hands. The image was probably from a movie I had just seen, *Mississippi Burning*. I did not take the bullet personally for the simple reason that I had been shot for the same reason the young black man had been killed in that Mississippi town in the 1960s. It was the same reason that sent millions of Jews to the death chambers, that triggered the Tutsi massacre in Rwanda in 1994, the killing of thousands of Bosnians in 1995 in the Srebrenica region, or the hundreds of Palestinian minors in Gaza in January 2009. My history is only a fragment of a longer history of racism and hatred. I am one detail in the continuum of racial othering, of dehumanizing those who are of another colour, belief or culture. So how could I take it personally?

# 5
# Homelessness

> The man who finds his homeland sweet is still a tender beginner;
> he to whom every soil is as his native one is already strong;
> but he is perfect to whom the entire world is as a foreign land.
>
> Hugo of St. Victor,
> twelfth-century Augustinian mystic

> This life is a hospital where every patient is possessed
> with the desire to change beds; one man would like to
> suffer in front of the stove, and another believes that he
> would recover his health beside the window
>
> Charles Baudelaire

In the summer of 1995, I had to return to Iran. My father was sick and, since he still faced a travel ban, I had no choice but to go back to see him. Borders have followed him even into his late seventies. Even weak and ill, the borders forbade him to move. In the early 1990s, I asked him to apply for a passport. We believed that an old man would no longer be considered a danger to the state. We were wrong. The authorities, in reopening the case, revealed that there was a 'minor' problem in his file. They told my father that he had been subject to a travel ban even before the 1979 Revolution, during the reign of the Shah, and the post-revolutionary authorities required an explanation. My father had no idea as to the reason for the ban. The authorities said that until he explained why he had been banned from travelling under the Shah, they could not lift his travel ban under the rule of the Islamic Republic. The most painful and eeriest part of the Kafkaesque border bureaucracy in my father's case is that he – and most likely no-one else either, including the authorities themselves – does not know and will probably never know the reason for his travel ban. A forced immobility had been imposed on him.

So when he asked me to go back, I did not hesitate. As expected, I was arrested on arrival at the airport in Tehran. The border guard took my passport and kept me until I was released on bail. A week later in 'court' at the airport, I was sentenced to three years' jail for leaving the country illegally. Afterwards, however, I was told by the secretary that I could 'buy' my prison time – which I did. I was released but only got back my passport after a month. During the first night at the airport, I was interrogated by a police officer, who was very curious and suspicious about why I chose anthropology as my subject. Other young Iranians abroad usually studied medicine or technology. I gave him an introductory lecture on anthropology, with an emphasis on applied and action anthropology and Third World development. Surprisingly, he liked my speech. After that summer, my visits to Iran became more regular. However, every time I cross the border it feels like an exception. 'You made it this time, too,' I think.

The first night at our house in Isfahan, I woke up several times and thought I was dreaming. I could not believe I was *there*, at home. Yet return does not mean coming home. From the beginning, I felt that I was both insider and outsider. After eight years of absence, everything seemed unexpectedly familiar, from the inefficient bureaucracy to bargaining over a taxi-fare, and this gave me a feeling of belonging. But in the second week, I was struck by the fact that I was not familiar in the eyes of others. I often neglected the moral obligations our tribal tradition imposed on young men, obligations often opposed to the lifestyle I had acquired living outside Iran. I had changed more than I had realized. Lubkemann describes Zimbabweans' experience of displacement in South Africa, and how 'prolonged resettlement brings about profound transformation in social identities and organization, in socioeconomic practices and expectations and in social life strategies, all of which in turn modify refugees' own notion of where and what is "home"' (Lubkemann 2008:260).

The glorious homecoming of exiles is a subject of myth and saga. Sometimes homecoming is full of shame, rather than glory. On my further visits, I gradually realized that I was not a 'good enough' migrant. The idealized migrant is one whose commitment to home continuously manifests itself through social and economic investments, activities and performances (Lubkemann 2008). An idealized migrant demonstrates his or her attachment to home through social reproduction, for example, by marrying a local, buying a local house or starting a local business. My social investments in terms of writing, translating and giving occasional speeches when I was back, targeting academics in Tehran, mainly went unnoticed by my family and people in my village. Shame was inevitable. Once in my village, Sattar, an old man who had worked his whole adult life for my father and grandfather, asked me what I had accomplished all those years abroad (*kharej*). I said that I was a *mardomshenas* or anthropologist – *mardomshenasi* literally means 'knowing the people'. Sattar did not hide his disappointment: 'All those years and you know the people! I know the people, too. More than you. You should have become a doctor to cure our disease. Or at least a *mohandes* – engineer – to build a school for us. What good is "knowing the people" to us?'

My failure in the 'migratory performances' (Lubkemann 2008) expected by the home community was obvious. *Kharej* literally means 'outside' or 'abroad', but is mainly used to refer to the West. Referring solely to the wealthy and modern West, *kharej* and its adjective form *khareji* imply high quality and standards. Like the consumption of *khareji* goods, ideas of *kharej* are mobilized in the discourse on success, progress, wealth, health, aesthetics and even sexuality (see Khosravi 2008). The material attributes of the 'good life' in the West are also commonly imagined and held in high value by others, including Somalis (Horst 2006), Chinese (Teo 2003), Ghanaians (Martin 2007) and Eritreans (Treiber 2007).

*Kharej* for many Iranians has connotations of higher education. If you get a chance, in this case, to achieve wealth and advancement in terms of more practical and 'useful' education, and you do not use it in a way that is perceived as beneficial, not only to yourself but also to the people around you, you have betrayed them. The shame of failure in the 'migratory performances' has impeded Ramin from returning to Iran. Ramin was a friend from New Delhi. I met him again after 13 years in September 2001 in Amsterdam. Ramin was from a lower-middle-class family and had spent two years in India before ending up in the Netherlands, with the help of a *dal lal*, one year after my departure. His family got heavily into debt paying for his long journey. When I met him after 13 years, he was suffering from deep depression. When I asked him why he did not try to go back to his family in Tehran, he answered that it was because of shame: 'I have neither a good education nor capital. How can I go back with empty hands [*daste khali*]?'

## When home fades away

As time goes by the dreams fade. The map of Isfahan I drew in room 404 in Hotel Shalimar represented a losing struggle against fading memories. I have forgotten. Memories fail and absence leads to ignorance. I was not at home when my parents got old and when my younger sister, only 12 years old when I left, became a beautiful young woman. I was not there when my nephews and nieces came of age. I was not there when my aunts and my grandfather passed away. In all the wedding parties and funeral ceremonies, 'my place was empty'. In my relatives' family albums, there are only a few pictures of me, all from my childhood. In the gigantic cemetery on the outskirts of Isfahan, I cannot find the graves of my beloved ones. I do not know a lot of things, trivial things, but things that are still crucial to the feeling of belonging. Ignorance makes me an alien in the country of my childhood. I spent only the first two decades of my life with my parents. I do not know them as does my brother, who has lived with them almost five decades, his whole life. I do not know what diseases they have suffered from. I was not there when they were hospitalized. They did not tell me for fear of making me anxious – nor did I tell them of my own suffering for the same reason. In our care, we excluded ourselves from each other's lives. My parents truly know my brother. They have seen him both sad and happy. They know how he has suffered from a kidney problem and how he gradually began wearing glasses for reading. Who knows me? My parents do not know about Hotel Shalimar, nor do they know about the Laser Man. I simply could not tell them. Exile has made me an alien in Sweden and a foreigner in Iran.

It is the predicament of 'double absence' (Sayad 1999), not having a place in either society. My 'double absence' reveals itself clearly in my linguistic impotence. I lack some domain vocabularies. For instance, I do not know names of many flowers, trees, vegetables, insects and fishes in any language, neither in Farsi nor in Swedish or English. I never learned them in Iran or have forgotten them after my long absence. And in other languages, simply stated, I have never reached that point of fluency.

In Canto 26 of *Inferno*, Dante tells a different story of Odysseus's return from that told by Homer. Certainly influenced by his own exile in Florence, Dante says that Odysseus's return to Ithaca was only the beginning of a new journey to the Western seas. His longing for Ithaca, the archetype of the longing for home, was not quenched by going back. Ironically, going back to Ithaca – where he was unknown, unrecognized by everybody except his faithful dog Argos – marked the beginning of his homelessness. I bore the burden of exile by harbouring the dream of going back home. Finding out that I was even alien at home marked the beginning of an eternal homelessness. Since then, in Hugo of St. Victor's words, 'the entire world is as a foreign land'. One reason I could not be at home in Iran, or did not want to recognize it as my home, is the xenophobia and racism towards immigrants I observe there, particularly towards undocumented Afghans.

## Biographical vignette

I was back in Isfahan in the summer of 2007. At a family gathering, the host asked everyone to donate some money for a clandestine Afghan couple who were the caretakers of a building in her neighbourhood. When the party was coming to its end and almost all guests had gone, the host handed me the collected donations in a packet, together with some food, and asked me to give them to the Afghan couple. They lived in a small room in a basement garage, just a few buildings away in a modern luxurious, multi-storey building. It was almost midnight and they did not open the door until I told them who had sent me. Khalil opened the port. He was alone; his wife, Sakina, had probably stayed in their room. I handed over the packet of money and the food, and asked whether I could come back again to talk to him about their situation.

I visited him a few days later with more money collected at another family gathering. Embarrassed, he explained that his wife was sick and apologized that he could not offer proper hospitality to me, his guest. We sat on the staircase in the yard and drank tea that his wife, Sakina, had made. Khalil was young, maybe 25 years old or so – he did not know his exact age. He came to Iran in search of work in the late 1990s. Labels such as 'asylum seeker', 'refugee', 'immigrant' and 'undocumented migrant' were unfamiliar to him. He was, in his own words, a simple 'Afghan worker' (*kargar-e Afghan*). A few years earlier in the vicinity of Zeinabieh, with its concentration of Afghan immigrants, he met Sakina with whom he fell in love. 'Does Sakina mean the one who consoles?' I asked Khalil. He smiled and said, 'That is why I married her'.

Sakina was born to undocumented Afghan parents in Isfahan. She belonged to the large second generation of undocumented Afghans in Iran, born into a clandestine life and living her whole life as one who does not exist. Her birth is recorded in neither Iran nor Afghanstan, and her life has been circumscribed by this double absence. Since she was not registered, she could not go to school or get a job. Obviously, their marriage was not registered either. They were outside the applicable norms, rules and rights. They inhabited a space of *non-existence* (Coutin 2003), a space of invisibility, exploitation, exclusion and violence. In this condition, norms and rules taken for granted by all *citizens* cease to apply. This state of irregularity affects even the smallest aspects of life. All everyday activities are 'illegalized', from housing and work to physical mobility. Undocumented immigrants lack not only the right to healthcare, education, police protection and work, but also the right to social relations and freedom of movement in public spaces.

Khalil and Sakina were caught in a condition of 'deportability' (De Genova 2002), of invisible detention. Constant risk of deportation – not the act of deportation itself – imposed a forced immobility on them. Fear is embedded in the condition of deportability. It is always 'in the air' around an undocumented migrant, and was a recurrent theme to which my informants in Sweden, Khalil and Sakina in Iran, Frank in Istanbul returned. Fear of arrest and deportation leaves one no peace. The same fear of deportation Willen found among undocumented migrants in Tel Aviv was embodied by my informants, so that every act of physical mobility was shaped by various 'somatic modes of attention' (Willen 2007:17). Spatially embodied fear were evident in the movements of undocumented migrants in public places. In an agoraphobic manner, they stayed away from crowds and public places; all my informants in Sweden avoided the city centre and places of entertainment, such as amusement parks, museums and large shopping centres. At night, they stayed indoors unless they had to go out to work, to minimize the risk of apprehension. This spatially embodied fear leads to a constant feeling of being under surveillance, which functions as a disciplining mechanism. The condition of 'illegality' demands unconditional submission, and my informants took great care not to do anything 'wrong'. Undocumented migrants cannot afford to make mistakes (see Rouse 1991; De Genova 2002:429). For example, my informants never used the underground without a ticket or leaned on cars for fear of the alarm going off. They did not object to their low wages. The condition of 'illegality' results in such docility that, in the words of a young undocumented Bangladeshi man in Stockholm, one 'does not even dare to jaywalk'. Ironically, the undocumented migrant exemplifies the impeccable citizen.

In the condition of 'illegality', even time has a different meaning and rhythm (see Willen 2007). Ehsan, a young undocumented Kurdish man in Stockholm, hated all weekdays and most of all Mondays. In his view, on the first day of the week all 'ordinary' people started a meaningful week of work while he did not: Mondays represented 'moving forward', while he just 'remained at the same point'. His time was not that of 'ordinary' people. Many other informants also used terms like 'dead time' or 'a time of death' when talking about their lives; they did not consider their time of hiding as part of life but rather a time of non-existence.

Khalil's and Sakina's fear of deportation was well-founded. The relatively tolerant Iranian policy towards the presence of Afghan immigrants in the 1980s changed drastically in the mid-1990s. In the 1980s, Iran had opened its borders to displaced Afghans who had fled Soviet occupation. The Iranian state regarded them as members of the Islamic *umma* (community). During the eight-year-long war with Iraq and the ensuing 'Construction Era', the Afghans made a cheap and docile labour force. Afghan people have been exposed to systematic discrimination by the authorities and to tangible xenophobia in everyday life. Afghan immigrants and their children are blamed for almost all social and other problems in Iran, from unemployment and increasing criminality to the spread of disease. The story of the plight and suffering of Afghans in Iran remains largely untold. It is probably best illustrated in the cinema, in films such as *Bicycle Ran, Baran, Heiran* and *Djomeh*. *Heiran* is a striking story of a young Iranian girl in love with an undocumented Afghan man. Their love, and later on their child, are regarded as illegitimate by both the authorities and the girl's family. The man is arrested and, along with a large group of other Afghan immigrants, is to be deported by bus to Afghanistan. The girl and the child follow the bus to the border. The scene of separation, when the man sends kisses to his beloved and his child from the other side of the window, when the border forbids connection, touching, love, illustrates the ruthlessness and naked brutality of borders.

In the case of refugees, Iran has signed the 1951 Convention and its 1967 Protocol, but maintains reservations regarding many of the covered rights, such as 'freedom of movement' and 'right to work'. Afghan refugees, however, are allowed to work in 16 menial job categories, such as brick-making and animal husbandry. Since the early 1990s, the Iranian state has used Afghan immigrants as political tools in relation to the Taliban and later on with the US-backed new government in Afghanstan. The mass deportation of hundreds of thousands of Afghans within a very short time proved an effective political strategy. The first repatriation program for Afghans, which had already begun in 1992, resulted in the 'return' of 600,000 registered Afghans in 1993. The pursuit and expulsion of undocumented Afghans intensified after the American occupation of Afghanstan, and the intensified mass removal of documented and undocumented Afghan nationals began in 2002. According to the Iranian Office for Foreigners, nearly 8000 Afghans were leaving Iran daily in the spring of 2004 (Mehr News, 22 January 1384/2005). More than 4.7 million Afghans voluntarily returned or were forcibly deported from Iran and Pakistan between 2002 and 2006 (IDMC 2008).

To accelerate the 'return' program, Iranian authorities embarked on still harsher policies against Afghan immigrants. For instance, employers of undocumented Afghans are subject to heavy fines and imprisonment. Services to Afghans, including healthcare and education, have been drastically reduced. Furthermore, residence in and even travel through much of the country has become unlawful for Afghans (BBC Persian, 18 October 2008). At the same time, the official media started attacking Afghans, claiming that their presence endangers the safety and wellbeing of Iranian society (*Jamejamonline*, 10 October 2006). The mass removal process has generally been atrocious and violent. For instance, the shanty houses of Afghans on the outskirts of Shiraz were destroyed by bulldozers. People were herded into trucks and removed, and at least one death during the mass deportation has been reported (BBC Persian, 3 May 2007fixed).

Return brings disastrous consequences for many Afghan returnees. Many cannot return to their hometowns or villages due to armed conflict. Returnees usually find their homes ruined and their lands occupied; they face serious problems with landmines, they lack access to healthcare and their children have no access to schooling (Jazayery 2002). Consequently, repatriation for many Afghans means secondary displacement in urban refugee camps. The repatriation of a huge number of refugees in a short period undermines stability, the peace process and development projects. This is primarily because the mass removal of Afghans from Iran and Pakistan cuts off remittances, which are the livelihood of many poor families (remittances from Iran have been around USD 500 million annually, equivalent to 6 per cent of Afghanstan's GDP). In addition, the increasing number of camp refugees puts increasing pressure on already limited resources.

For all these reasons, Khalil and Sakina chose to be as invisible as possible. Sakina had been pregnant a year earlier. She was ill almost all the time, but they were afraid to seek prenatal care. She gave birth at home, and Sakina almost died because of birth complications. However, the child, their first, was born dead in the basement of the luxury building. Khalil said that she was pregnant again and that they were considering returning to Afghanstan despite all the difficulties. They could not imagine losing this child, too.

When I gave Khalil the phone number of a cousin who is a physician, he said: 'One cannot be a guest for too long a time'. I was still thinking of what to say when he thanked me, as the host, for the years he had lived in Iran. I was not sure who was host and who was guest: Sakina was born on the same soil as I, but had lived even longer than I on that soil. Yet she is still seen as a guest. The idea of immigrant as guest is a metaphor, but people have forgotten that it is a metaphor (Rosello 2001:3). Immigrants and even their children are regarded as guests. One is regarded as a guest as long as one is regarded as an immigrant. An immigrant cannot be a host for the simple reason that she or he is a guest whose presence is expected to be only temporary. A guest is always a stranger; there is an asymmetric power relationship between host and guest.

This relationship is violent. It requires a definite gratitude. Guests are expected to display their gratitude for being tolerated. Naturalization ceremonies, which may include kissing the flag, manifest the expectation of gratitude. Even my undocumented informants never forget to thank the Swedish people and Swedish society when they get a chance.

One of my informants, an Iranian woman in her early forties, was granted asylum after five years of waiting. When the Migration Board officer announced the good news in his office, she threw herself on the ground and kissed his feet. It was a striking and touching scene of subordination expressed in terms of the guest–host relationship. In the case of undocumented migrants and refugees, the guest's gratitude is nourished by a sense of shame. When Khalil thanked me and said that he could not be a guest for too long a time, he was revealing his embarrassment. Khalil saw himself as an uninvited, unwelcome guest, an undesirable person. He was embarrassed by and felt guilty at his presence on the Iranian side of the border – as I did in Sweden. In our meetings, his body language, his averted gaze and his way of speaking when he addressed me manifested shame. I recognized myself, my shame in Sweden, in him and his shame. Shame is imposed by the host on the uninvited guest: by the excluding gaze of the media, politicians and bureaucrats, by an exposing gaze that deprives migrants of their history, emotions, personality and intellect, transforming them into undesirable aliens.

Khalil's body language and words manifested how profoundly and forcefully 'illegality' can be embodied and internalized. The violence inherent in the condition of 'illegality' expresses itself in the internalization of 'human inequalities' (see Holmes 2007), seeing oneself as inferior only because of not having a paper, a passport, a stamp. To Khalil, though, it was *my* home, in which Khalil was seen by others and by himself as the unwanted guest. For me to *be at* home in Iran, to *have* a home, means prolonging the plight and suffering of Khalil and Sakina. Being at home means belonging, but it also means constructing borders and excluding the other. Any kind of group identification constructs the social category of the other.

Homes are primarily sites of exclusion, not inclusion. The notion of the home nourishes racism and xenophobia. The German Jewish philosopher, Theodor Adorno, himself exiled by the Nazis, believed that 'it is part of morality not to be at home in one's home' (2002 [1974]:39). To follow Adorno is to stand away from *home*, not take it for granted, and to defamiliarize it to realize the discrepancies between the concept and what it actually produces. One of these discrepancies is that the borders that 'enclose us within the safety of familiar territory, can also become prisons' (Said 2001 [1984]:188). Unsurprisingly, a similar warning about the implications of *home* can be read in *The Burrow*, the last and unfinished short story by Kafka, a homeless Jew. An unidentified, mole-like creature, in fear of an imagined enemy, digs an inexpugnable burrow consisting of multiple tunnel systems. As the animal hears the sound of the 'enemy' coming closer and closer, it digs deeper and deeper. The burrow, however, is gradually revealed to have become a trap with no way out. The enemy does not exist outside the burrow, and by the end of the story, the animal realizes that the sounds are coming from *inside* the burrow. Possibly, the enemy *is* the burrow. Giorgio Agamben asks whether our homes, the nation-state system, will in the end 'be only lethal traps for the very peoples that were supposed to inhabit them' (2000:139).

The romantic combination of cosmopolitanism and 'being at home', referred to as the 'great combination' (Löfgren 1999:24) and common among Western middle-class white academics, is just an illusion. The notions of cosmopolitanism and 'being at home' are incompatible for the simple reason that the notion of home disavows the basic elements of what is called cosmopolitanism, namely unconditional hospitality. It is only in homelessness that genuine hospitality becomes possible. Homelessness means not recognizing anywhere as home. Only in that condition is humanity not territorialized and can the plagues inherent in the nation-state system vanish and the 'botanical' way of thinking about human beings, in terms of roots, and the uncritical link between individuals and territory fade away. Exiled homelessness designates de-territoriality, discontinuity, inconsistency and interruption, all in contrast to the botanical image of national identity. Homelessness as a paradigm, as a way of being in the world, as a lifestyle, as ethical and aesthetic normativity opens the door to accepting the other as she *is*, not as how we want her to be. Only when *home* has vanished and humanity is no longer territorialized, only then, there will be a chance for humanity.

One year later in 2008, during a short visit in Iran, I looked everywhere for Khalil and Sakina. Like many other undocumented migrants I have met as friends or informants, they too were gone without a trace.

# 6
# We Borders

The invisible border, or in Balibar's words, the 'colour bar', waylays you everywhere and nowhere. It startles, humiliates, hurts you. It pierces your soul. The border subtly sets the rock rolling down, forcing you to start rolling it up again.

On 18 September 2006, I arrived at Bristol airport, along with a few colleagues from Stockholm University. I was the convener of a workshop on 'irregular migration in Europe' at the biannual conference of the European Association of Social Anthropologists (EASA). After passing through immigration control, I was stopped by a security officer who let my blond fellow travellers pass. In the middle of a narrow corridor, a mini interrogation began, which lasted half an hour. 'Bordering is selective and targeted' (Rumford 2006:164). My status as a Swedish citizen disappeared at the racialized border because of my face. I answered questions about myself, my education, work and the purpose of my visit to Bristol. Then the officer asked about my parents, where they lived and what they did. I was unwilling to give her any kind of information about my elderly parents. How could I recount the violence against my father, persecuted by Iranian authorities for decades? How could I disclose my mother's life to an officer I did not know? What did my mother have to do with global terrorism? Once again, in the middle of a narrow corridor of the Bristol Airport, my private life was forced into the public domain. When I refused to answer her questions about my parents, she threatened to detain me first for nine hours and then, if necessary, for nine days according to the Anti-Terrorism Act. The officer handed me a leaflet on the Anti-Terrorism Act, according to which I was obliged to answer any question the officer asked; in case of non-collaboration, I could be prosecuted under paragraph 18(1) of Schedule 7 of the Terrorism Act of 2000.

I protested that she had targeted me because of my 'Middle Eastern' look and that her selection of suspicious people was racist. She did not even deny it, saying 'You want to kill us. We have to protect ourselves'. Needless to mention that her 'you' here referred to me and terrorists. Hearing this, I decided to return to Sweden at once. This was not an option either until I had answered the questions, I was informed. Put into a petrifying immobility, I could move neither in nor out. I was indistinguishable from the border; I *was* the border. When she realized that I had decided to be detained rather than answer her questions about my parents, she wished me a pleasant time in Bristol! Suddenly, I was a full EU citizen again with a surplus of mobility rights and freedom of movement. My legal status as an EU citizen was apparently not fixed, but rather situational, conditional and unconfirmed. I am a quasi-citizen whose rights can be suspended in a state of emergency. I am included and at the same time excluded. This is exactly how the contemporary border regime operates.

I have been a Swedish citizen since 1995. Today, with a Swedish passport in hand, I can cross most borders without major difficulty. There is, however, one border that categorically mistrusts the relationship between me and my passport, and thereby impedes, delays and holds me back. Ironically, it is the Swedish border. It is not just a physical or administrative frontier, but pre-eminently a 'colour bar' (Balibar 2002:78). When returning to Sweden, the border requires me to live up to my passport. While others pass through, I am asked some 'innocent' questions to prove that I do speak Swedish, that I can identify myself with my passport. Ironically, the same authority that approved my citizenship and issued a passport in my name mistrusts the relationship between my body and my passport.

Through 'inclusive exclusion' (Agamben 1998:17), undesirable people – 'illegal' migrants, refugees and quasi-citizens – are positioned on the threshold between *in* and *out*. Their experience is indistinct from the operation of the nation-state and their very existence is indistinct from the border (Raj 2006). By rebordering politics, the sovereign power does not merely exclude undesirable people, but penalizes and regulates them, by immobilizing them in detention centres, by ignominious and terrifying threats of deportation, or by racialized internal border control – all of which turns the citizen into a quasi-citizen. As Balibar puts it, 'some borders are no longer situated at the borders at all' in the geographical or political sense of the term (2002:84). Borders have become invisible borders, situated everywhere and nowhere. Hence, undesirable people are not expelled by the border, they are forced to *be* border (ibid.).

I am the border. I can, however, enjoy my quasi-citizenship from time to time, when conditions allow it. My informants, stateless, undocumented, failed asylum seekers, are constantly caught in the position of *being* the border. In this section, I will shift the focus from my own journeys to my informants' and to the process of making borders of people.

In October 2004, I was in Frankfurt to attend a conference. I felt bad because Vartan, my key informant in my research into undocumented migrants in Sweden, had just been arrested by the police and was in a detention centre awaiting deportation. Vartan was a middle-aged Armenian man who had lived clandestinely in Sweden after his request for asylum was rejected in 1998. Vartan was my first informant. He was from a working-class background, and his elderly mother survived thanks to the small amount of money Vartan sent back home. A deportation was not immediately planned and I was sure I could visit him after coming back from the conference. On my last day in Frankfurt, just before jumping into a taxi to the airport, I called the detention centre, but they said that Vartan was not there any more. I called a mutual friend. He said that Vartan had been escorted by two policemen to the airport earlier that day, deported to Armenia via Frankfurt. The irony was that at the same time as I was flying to Stockholm, he was in an airplane headed to Frankfurt.

I would have shared the destiny of Vartan and many other of my informants if I had sought asylum in the 2000s. When I came to Sweden, Europe had not yet raised its walls. Today my informants, fleeing formidable wars in Afghanstan, Somalia and Iraq, are facing the restrictive asylum regime that has emerged since the late 1990s in Europe. Vartan was the first but not the last of my informants to fall victim to this new regime. Throughout my fieldwork, many people, both informants and others I knew from the field, were expelled from Sweden.

Detention and deportation are the bodily sanctions imposed by the current migration regime. What is brutal about the confinement of asylum seekers is that these people are *not* being held on criminal charges, but on their claim of having experienced persecution (Welch and Schuster 2005). Due to the harmonization of migration and asylum policy in the European Union, the relatively generous Swedish policy towards asylum seekers has gradually become more restrictive over the first years of the new century. Accordingly, immigration penality, by excluding and expelling undesired non-citizens, has become central to the asylum regime in Sweden. Such immigration penality arose as a result of the current security panic associated with migration. The security–migration nexus emerged in the early 1990s after the end of the Cold War (Weiner 1993), but was radicalized after the terror attacks in New York in September 2001 (Tirman 2004). Consequently, immigration policies have become increasingly criminalized (Welch 2002) and immigration governance has increasingly been implemented by criminalization. 'Governing through criminalization' makes crime and punishment the institutional context, whereby a criminal population (the poor, 'illegal' immigrants, asylum seekers, 'terrorists') are constructed and excluded (Simon 2007; see also Rose 1999:259). The justification for governing through criminalization is to protect citizens from the 'threats' posed by the newly 'criminal' population.

Criminals – poor people, homeless people, undocumented immigrants and unidentified asylum seekers – are presented as threats to the wellbeing of the social body. Immigration penality 'constitutes and enforces borders, polices non-citizens, identifies those deemed dangerous, diseased, deceitful, or destitute, and refuses them entry or casts them out' (Pratt 2005:1). Targeting undesirable aliens, governing through criminalization, is conducted by enforcing harsher external and internal border controls, confinement and forced deportation.

Lamin, a 25-year-old man from Guinea, left his country when he was 16 years old to seek refuge in Europe. Assisted by a human smuggler, he came to Germany, where he applied for asylum. His application was rejected, and he fled to the Netherlands but was not granted asylum there either. For nine years, he was tossed back and forth between different European countries. In the spring of

2001, he applied for asylum in Sweden. After a year-and-a-half wait, he was rejected. He borrowed a friend's passport and tried to get to the USA, where he was arrested and spent three months in prison before being sent back to Sweden in November 2003. At his return, he was detained. In December 2003, he was deported to Guinea, but since he lacked identity documents, he was sent back to Sweden and was again locked up in the Migration Board's detention centre. He spent two years in various detention centres and even in prison. He actually prefers prison to detention centres: 'There you know what you're in for and for how long. Here there's no time limit. Not for me at any rate – I'm black, that's my skin colour. No one has been inside for as long as I have. A criminal knows what he's in for, but I don't.'

Lamin was detained for over two years before he was released at the end of 2005 under the new, temporary law on asylum. He had been locked up for 25 months without having committed a crime.

The removal system is based on a distinction between who is desirable and deserving and who is not, between those whose lives are useful (legitimate) and those whose lives are wasted (illegitimate) (Bauman 2004:33). 'Immigration imprisonment', as Jonathan Simon calls it, forms part of the general prison system but differs from it in significant ways (Simon 1998).

The modern prison is assigned the task of administering its inmates' lives in order to foster 'docile and useful bodies' (Foucault 1977). It is based on a 'caring' and 'saving' policy that disciplines the inmates so that they may become beneficial and productive citizens in a market economy. The immigration detention centre, by contrast, is a pre-modern prison – nothing more than a site for the punishment and permanent removal of 'wasted' bodies. The removal system regulates national 'purity' by confining and deporting undesirable non-citizens who are seen as 'economically marginal and politically dangerous' (Simon 1998:603). While prison is associated with 'disciplining' and 'normalization' (Foucault 1977), detention is associated with exposing undesirable non-citizens to abandonment or even death.

The authorities claim that a detention centre is not a prison and does not aim to punish; if that were so, then 'the detainees would have certain due process rights' (Dow 2007:534). While a criminal knows why he or she is imprisoned and knows for how long, a detainee like Lamin can be held for no reason and for no time limit. Yet this does not mean that, as another detained informant once said, 'there is no law for us [detainees]'. As a detainee, my informant's destiny is determined by the law, which has, nevertheless, excluded him. There is law but it is not accessible.

Immigration penality is seen by my informants (see Khosravi 2009a) as a strategy of deterrence for people en route to Europe. Alongside 'immigration penality', another pivotal feature of the harsh current asylum is interception measures, that is, more border controls, to impede the mobility of undesirable people to Europe.

## The walls indeed now stand high

One not unexpected consequence of harsher border control has been the increasing danger and cost of human smuggling. My informants' testimonies convey differences between their journey experiences and mine. The smugglers they dealt with differ drastically from Homayoun, Nour and many other *dal lals* I met on my journey. Harsher border control has resulted in more sophisticated human smuggling operations. Current global human smuggling requires more information, transnational connections, and expertise than before. 'Amateur' smugglers like Homayoun, Mahmood and Nour have been driven out of the market by more professional actors with more organized and transnational networks.

Migrants pay the price of harsher border control not only with their money, but also with their lives. The brutality of human smuggling has increased with the tightening of border control. Since smuggling people by air has become almost impossible, smugglers now use land and sea routes. To circumvent the most controlled border sections, smuggling routes have been relocated to more inaccessible and dangerous areas. By closing the most accessible sections of borders, 'geography would do the rest' (Cornelius 2005:779). And it does. Operation Gatekeeper on the Mexico–USA border, launched in 1994, resulted in the relocation of illicit border crossings from urban areas of San Diego County, California, to remote mountains and desert locations in western Arizona. Consequently, the number of border-crossing deaths has doubled since 1995 (GAO-06-770, also Cornelius 2001).

'The fortified US border with Mexico has been more than 10 times deadlier to migrants from Mexico during the past nine years than the Berlin Wall was to East Germans through its 28-year existence' (Cornelius 2005:783). Migrant fatalities have also increased along European–African borders (Carling 2007). The dumping of groups of migrants from leaky boats into the Mediterranean Sea is recurrent news.

Migrant fatalities elsewhere in the world – albeit neglected by states and NGOs, and rarely covered by the mainstream media – are often greater in number and more tragic. The Gulf of Aden, in the Arabian Sea between the south coast of the Arabian Peninsula and the Horn of Africa, is the scene of the most devastating tragedies of migrant death in modern times. Every year, tens of thousands of Somalis and Ethiopians try to cross the Gulf in the hope of finding better lives. They pay between USD 50 and USD 200 to be placed in overloaded boats on a hellish journey. Many of these passengers never reach their destinations: they are beaten to death and thrown overboard by the smugglers. According to the UNHCR, almost 80,000 people plied this atrocious journey in 2007 and 2008, 2350 of whom drowned (UNHCR 2009). Somali diplomatic sources in Yemen, however, claim that more than 3500 Somalis drowned in 2008 alone (*Asharq Al-Awsat*, 4 December 2008).Most of the deaths, however, occur not very far off the Yemen coast. Like along the Africa–Spain border (cf. Carling 2007:329), migrant death in the Gulf of Aden often occurs during interception measures. Fearing detection, the smugglers throw the migrants, who usually cannot swim, into the sea. The increasing border control by the coastguard patrols results in smugglers taking more dangerous sea routes (*Yemen Times*, 21 February 2007). The proportional relationship between increasing border control and migrant fatalities is conspicuous and undeniable.

To survive unauthorized border crossing in the present border regime, physical strength is required, so it is more likely that only young, healthy and strong people will risk such a journey. Borders thus make a selection. The new border regime favours 'young, fit men and discourages women, children, and old people' (Carpenter 2006:170). Even in the case of irregular migration, borders enforce a social sorting. Denying education and health services to undocu-mented children and prenatal care to undocumented women, alongside a border regime that favours young healthy men over women and children, has resulted in the defeminization of irregular migration. For instance, the current Mexican–US border policy recalls the Bracero Program, which aimed to provide the American economy with cheap male labour between 1942 and 1964 (Carpenter 2006).

Harsher border control has also increased the price of human smuggling, making it a more lucrative business than before. In fact, today it is one of the most profitable illegal businesses (GCIM 2005). For instance, since the implementation of Operation Gatekeeper, the proportion of migrants using *coyotes* rose from 15 to 41 per cent (Cornelius 2005:783). The human smuggling fee has increased on the Mexico–USA border as well. While before Operation Gatekeeper, the average fee for being smuggled into California was USD 143, the fee in 2004 was USD 2000 (Cornelius 2005:783). The average fee for smuggling a person from China to the USA was USD 23,000 in 1988 (Chin 1999:37), but by 2005, the same journey could cost as much as USD 70,000 (Petros 2005).

In 1988, I paid USD 2000 to be sent to Sweden from India, but in 2005 an informant paid almost four times more for the same journey. While in 1988 it cost USD 2500 to be smuggled from India to Canada, according to a *dal lal*, the 2005 fee was between USD 12,000 and USD 20,000. Similarly, the profit accrued from smuggling a migrant has also increased, by more than tenfold. Mahmood, a *dal lal* in New Delhi and a close friend of Nour's, later told me that of the USD 2000 I paid Nour, half would have gone for the ticket and USD 500 to the airport officials. The passport itself was forged and did not cost him anything. Nour probably earned USD 500 from me. In contrast, a smuggler today can earn almost USD 7000 per migrant from Pakistan to Europe (Koser 2008).

Multiplying these figures by the hundreds of thousands of people smuggled across borders each year, it becomes clear that human smuggling is today one of the most profitable illegal businesses (Koser 2008), comparable to drug smuggling. However, the smugglers I knew from Karachi and New Delhi are far from rich today.

Mahmood runs a small framing store in Toronto. Another one I knew from Cantt Station drives a cab in Stockholm. The Armenian photo 'doctor' in Karachi, who forged my passport, got a degree in civil engineering and now works at an IT company in London. Nour left Canada in the late 1990s, when he realized that he could not find any work except hard manual labour. He has lived from time to time in Russia and Afghanstan dealing in rugs. Pooya from New Delhi managed a small Persian restaurant in Toronto for many years. In the summer of 2008 he was unemployed and planning to move to Europe. Amir, a *dal lal* I met during my research, has been in prison in Sweden since the late 1990s and officially has no property or capital, according to the police. Amir, however, is different from all other human smugglers I have ever met.

## Biographical vignette

### Through the eyes of an existentialist human smuggler

The best-known *dal lal* among Iranians, Iraqis and Kurds is undoubtedly Amir Heidari, born in 1953 to Kurdish parents in Iran. Over more than two decades, tens of thousands of asylum seekers reached Europe through the agency of his organization. He had a good reputation for honesty and professionalism.

I interviewed him twice in prison in Sweden. First in May 2004 when he was serving a two-year sentence for falsifying documents and then in June 2009 when he was serving a four-year sentence for 'human smuggling'. I use his real name here because he wanted me to. Moreover, he has talked openly about his work in the mass media: he is proud to be a *dal lal*. The day before our meeting in May 2004, I received a call from a friend of Amir's who told me that Amir had invited me to have breakfast with him. He had prepared a simple but enjoyable breakfast table in the meeting room of the prison. In June 2009 he had prepared a tasty Kurdish meal for lunch.

*Shahram*: Tell me about your parents.
*Amir*: My father was an army officer before the 1979 Islamic Revolution. He was an idealist and supported Mohammad Mossadegh's democratic movement in the 1950s, for which he paid a high price. My mother is a housewife and lives here in Sweden.
*Shahram*: Why did you become a *dal lal*?
*Amir*: Kurds have always lived under political oppression and thus become familiar with social and political issues

early in life. After the 1979 Revolution, I became a political activist. I was 26 years old and joined a socialist movement as a guerrilla. I was shot and received injuries to my legs. In 1980, I was sent to Sweden via Turkey for treatment. Kurdish people were rejected by every country. This made me angry, so I went back to Turkey to help my people. Thousands of Kurdish refugees were trapped in Turkey and could be deported to Iran any day. We had to do something. I asked for help from the United Nations in Ankara, from the embassies of Western countries to pressure the Turkish state not to deport Kurds – in vain. So what about all those nice words on human rights we had heard from the West? I realized soon that no one would help us. I started my movement, which has not finished yet. I decided to send people in need to safety.

Shahram:   Can you say how you did your work then?

Amir:   The main problem we faced was lack of money. Most Kurds could not afford a ticket. So I started a carpet business in Istanbul. The profit from each carpet was used to send a Kurd to Europe. In the early 1980s, it was easy to send people to Europe. We more or less only paid for the ticket.

Shahram:   What about passports, border police and airport authorities?

Amir:   Many had passports. I just forged the stamps that were needed. The police did not care at the beginning, but later they started demanding money from us. Starting in 1984. And soon all the others were demanding money too – the travel agencies, the airport authorities. Everybody wanted a piece of the cake.

Shahram:   And this meant more expenses for the migrants?

Amir:   Yes. We used to get boarding cards without any difficulties, but then we were asked to pay USD 200 or USD 300 for each boarding card. Travel agencies did the same. They demanded money to issue the tickets. And so on. So the journey became almost USD 1000 more expensive.

Shahram:   Who were your clients?

Amir: Most were Kurds or political activists. The people I sent were from simple backgrounds. Some of them had never travelled by air before. Once I told a person he should tear up the passport and ticket 30 minutes after departure. I showed him the gate and went to the coffee shop. Suddenly, he appeared before me and said that he could not get on board. He had already torn up the passport and the ticket before departure! I sent him on again with a new passport and a new ticket. I bore all these costs myself. I felt I was responsible for these people. For me, it was part of the Kurdish movement, not a business. I helped only political activists.

Shahram: But you helped others than Kurds and political activists, too?

Amir: After a while, the carpet business was no longer profitable. So I started to send non-political people for money. My philosophy was to take more from one who had money and send one who had no money for free. I learnt this from the Swedish tax model. I said this in court. The judge and others laughed but did not believe me. They argued that since I had no other job, I must have lived on the money from this business. They called this profit. So if this is true, what about the Red Cross? It pays its employees to work, is this also profit?

Shahram: How much did you charge in the 1980s?

Amir: For the whole way from Iran to Sweden I charged USD 3500. This included smuggling from Iran to Turkey, expenses for accommodation and food during the transit period and then smuggling to Sweden.

Shahram: And how much do you charge now for the same journey?

Amir: USD 6000.

Shahram: How do you work from here [i.e., prison]?

Amir: I am like an architect. I just show them what to do. After so many years, I know how the police think.

Shahram: Who are 'they'?

Amir: The people who work with me.

Shahram: Did you work alone before?

| | |
|---|---|
| *Amir*: | No, I always worked with a group. We were just a handful of people at first, but by the late 1980s, I was working with up to 50 people from different places, from Iran and Turkey to Germany and Sweden. I had contact people in all major European cities. We had a well-organized and extended network by which we monitored the passenger throughout his or her journey. |
| *Shahram*: | Were they all Iranians or Kurds? |
| *Amir*: | No. I even had a Swedish woman in my group. Her job was to take passengers to Sweden from Denmark by car. She was blond and she would not attract suspicion as we would. |
| *Shahram*: | How did you recruit her? |
| *Amir*: | It was simple. I put a job ad in a local newspaper. It said that a Swedish woman was needed for a well-paid job. Many called me and I honestly told them what they would do. Some declined but one accepted. I never conceal what I do. |
| *Shahram*: | Why are there refugees? |
| *Amir*: | It is simple. The rich world plunders the poor world. When people have tried to make a change in politics and change the ruling regimes, the superpowers have intervened and stopped the democratic movements. In Chile, Allende was murdered and in Iran, Mossadegh was overthrown by the CIA. This is our situation. As long as there are plunderers [i.e., plundering countries], the plundered ones [i.e., refugees and migrants] will want to come and see where their wealth has ended up. |
| *Shahram*: | Once a *dal lal* in Pakistan told me that 'they cannot close the doors of the world'. |
| *Amir*: | This is true. It is like running water – if you block its way, it finds another. This is a law of nature. When a human being sees that she cannot live in one place, she moves to another place. Because she is intelligent. *Humane* law does not recognize any border. Borders are constructed by inhumane minds. I see no borders. Here is Sweden. I do not see Sweden – I see a globe. Everyone has the right to decide where she or he wants to live. ... |

| *Shahram*: | Is it why you became a *dal lal*? |
|---|---|
| *Amir*: | I am an existentialist. I mean Jean-Paul Sartre's philosophy. I believe individuals have free choice and by that responsibility. I believe that everyone should be able to do something with their lives. I am my own migration board. I work for those who are declined visas and passports. I work for anyone who has no passport, and with pleasure help them go wherever they want. You see birds and animals go everywhere they want. They do not have passports, so why should human beings? My thesis is to make the world more international. When the economy is globalized, it is foolish for human beings not to be globalized as well. We should help people get citizenships in other countries. We need a revolution. |
| *Shahram*: | Do you have any idea how many people you have helped on their journeys? |
| *Amir*: | I have no statistics, but I have helped more than 40,000 get to Sweden alone. |
| *Shahram*: | What do you think about the tragedies of migrant death on the Mediterranean Sea every day? |
| *Amir*: | I would never send people like that. I send people only by air. It has to be safe. |

He handed me a small yellow booklet. The title on the cover reads Rahnamaye taghazaye panahandegi (Guidelines for asylum seeking), and his name, as the author, comes under the title. Lower down on the cover, in smaller letters, it says that the booklet is free to asylum seekers. Written in Farsi, Amir gives basic information on the asylum process in 48 pages. The booklet gives guidelines on what to say to the police and immigration officers, and on how to make a reliable case. The booklet is also simple manual on how to behave in airports.

| *Amir*: | I have printed more than 7000 copies of this for my clients. It is important that people get correct information before they start their journeys. |
|---|---|

Amir said that he had revised the booklet and updated it in prison. He handed me sheaves of paper and politely asked whether I could read, comment on and even complete it. Later on, I saw the new updated edition on his website, www.amirheidari.com, which was shut down after he was arrested again in the summer of 2005.

*Shahram*:  What do you think about the term 'human smuggler'?

*Amir*:  I do not like being called a smuggler. I do not do it for money. I do it because I care. Sometimes one person pays me 5000 and I spend 15,000 on him. What smuggler would do that? If I wanted to get rich, I would be so today. If I moved rice instead of people from one country to another, I would have huge capital by now and not be here [i.e., in prison].

*Shahram*:  Are there any other states that would like to prosecute you?

*Amir*:  Yes. I have sent people to different countries. Many states want to put me in jail – Canada, Austria, England, Germany.

*Shahram*:  How long have you been in jail?

*Amir*:  In Sweden, 14 years altogether. I was imprisoned a shorter time in Denmark, Germany and Turkey. I do not mind. If you believe what you do is right.... Like Socrates. He paid a high price for his belief.... Sweden has a double standard of morality. I do what Raoul Wallenberg did during WW II. He was a hero who saved many Jews, but I am seen as a criminal. Do you remember how the Canadian embassy forged passports for the staff of the American embassy and saved them from the Iranian revolutionary forces in 1980? They are heros but I am a criminal.... In fact I do not smuggle people. I take them to the border where they can seek asylum. When they have sought asylum a refugee lawyer takes care of their cases. Why is my job a crime but not the lawyer's? We both have the same goal.

One month after the interview, in June 2004, Amir had served his sentence and was supposed to be released. However, he was moved to a detention section and was informed that he would be deported to Iran. His residence permit was withdrawn in 1995 but, due to the refugee status he had obtained in the 1980s, it was difficult to deport him. He was kept in detention for more than six months, waiting for deportation to Iran. In detention, he was isolated from others. He had no right to work or training. He ate his food alone in his cell and his contact with the outside world was cut off. He was treated the same as the most dangerous criminals. He was released for a brief time in the spring of 2005. I met him on 21 April 2005 at a demonstration for asylum rights organized by NGOs in Stockholm. We marched together. He said that his deportation order had not yet been cancelled. Later that year, Amir was arrested again and sentenced to four years in prison for holding 70 forged passports. What distinguishes him from other human smugglers are his anti-capitalist and anti-racist political beliefs, and his openness in talking about and defending his work. One more factor that distinguishes him from other *dal lals* is that he has continued to send people for more than two decades, despite his many prison sentences. While the common pattern is for a *dal lal* to work for several years, to save up enough capital for a safe and legal business, Amir kept sending people.

The meeting time in May 2004 was coming to an end, we were informed by a guard. Amir thanked me for visiting him. The guard opened the door. I put my recorder and notebook in my bag, and stretched my hand towards him. He, shaking my hand longer than usual, asked me whether I knew who the first human smuggler in history was. 'I do not know', I replied. 'Moses', Amir said.

As I write these words in October 2009, Amir, a 'human smuggler' who quotes Sartre and referred to Socrates, is serving a four-year sentence. His future is unknown. The day he is released he will be deported. As he has said, the authorities would never release him in Sweden again, for they know that he would start up his enterprise again to help migrants come to Sweden.

## Culture of disbelief

Asylum seekers are increasingly presented as 'not people who have a problem but as people who are a problem' (Joly et al. 1997). A public consensus has emerged that most of today's asylum seekers are 'bogus' refugees coming to Sweden only to scrounge benefits. 'Illegal' migrants and asylum seekers have become the 'folk devils' of the contemporary world (Cohen 2002). The image of refugees as being 'at risk' and deserving protection has been transformed into that of 'risky' refugees deserving confinement (Pratt 2005). According to the theory of the 'risk society', modern society is organized in response to real and imagined risks (Beck 1992). The categories of 'risky' refugees and 'risky' 'illegal' immigrants have been constructed in order to manage the insecurities caused by migration.

Alongside the tendency to criminalize migration, a culture of disbelief has emerged, which has infected the whole asylum system. In an environment of scepticism, the immigration authorities aim to *discredit* asylum claims rather than to establish their substance. The whole point of the asylum process is now to find discrepancies in the claimant's account, in order to discredit the authenticity of his or her grounds for asylum. Through the cases of my informants, I have witnessed how representations of a part – often a non-crucial one – can incredibly be used to discredit a whole account. One way to discredit an asylum applicant's story is to shift the focus from the reason for the asylum seeker's flight to the means of their journey, how they came to Sweden. For their own and others' safety, asylum seekers usually do not reveal all the details of their journey. Accordingly, the part of an asylum seeker's story in which it is easiest to find discrepancies is the story of his or her journey.

Gaps, inconsistencies and lack of detail about the journey are used to discredit the rest of the applicant's account, including the most significant part of it, namely, the reasons for flight. Furthermore, the only way into Fortress Europe for asylum seekers today is through human smuggling, so the criminalization of human smuggling has also criminalized asylum seekers. A telling example is provided by the utterances of one of Sweden's most famous politicians, Göran Johansson, who suggested in the autumn of 2007 that all smuggled asylum seekers who come to Sweden should be deported (*Dagens Nyheter*, 27 November 2007). Furthermore, a narrow interpretation of the concept of 'political' disqualifies most asylum seekers by labelling them 'bogus' or 'economic refugees'. The latter term is applied to someone who is said to have sought refugee status for purely economic reasons. In other words, their grounds for asylum are not seen as political, so their applications are rejected.

Is there any boundary between politics and the economy, especially in countries ruled by corrupt leaders? Poverty per se cannot be the main cause of migration for the simple reason that almost all poor people in Africa, Asia and Latin America are still in their places. The main cause of refugee migration is not poverty but corruption, inequality, class differences and unjust resource distribution. In most refugee sending societies, the boundary between politics and the economy is blurred. Not even forced displacement due to environmental disaster can be defined as completely 'natural' and 'non-political'. Famine, for example, is a political as well as an economic phenomenon (Turton 2003). While drought is a natural condition, famine is a consequence of political circumstances. People who starve in a famine in fact suffer from insufficient entitlement to food; they do not starve because no food is available (Sen 1981). They simply do not 'deserve' to have food. This is pre-eminently a political issue and not just an economic one.

To take another example, imagine that earthquakes of the same magnitude hit Tokyo and Kabul. The consequences in terms of human suffering would be incomparable. While we would probably see no asylum seekers from Tokyo, there would be a huge number from Kabul. The difference would relate to the political conditions in these two countries. The absence of a powerful and stable state and the absence of functioning infrastructure result in forced mass displacement. The state is always involved in refugee crises, either directly by violating human rights or indirectly by not being able to protect its citizens. Human suffering is always a political issue.

The culture of disbelief is based on the assumption of deservingness. To be granted asylum, one should deserve it by having suffered. Human suffering is usually assumed to be traceable on bodies. Bodily wounds are accepted as objective evidence of suffering and regarded as more reliable than words (Malkki 1997:232). Bodies are used as text. Evidence of torture on the body is used to evaluate the deservingness of the asylum seeker. Medical examinations, pictures of injured bodies and old scars are all used to prove the existence of suffering. Sometimes, indeed often, these wounds are insufficient evidence, for the simple reason that there is no way objectively to measure the suffering. How many fingers should one have lost in a police station in Jakarta to have suffered enough? How many times should one have been raped in Mogadishu to have suffered enough?

How much suffering is enough for someone to be deemed a deserving asylum applicant?

An assessment of the grounds for refusing an Ethiopian asylum seekers in the UK (Trueman 2009) illustrates explicitly how 'not enough' suffering underlies the refusals. In one case, rape was not 'severe enough' to be deemed sufficient grounds:

> For the reasons set out in the following paragraphs, I do not find the core of the Appellant's claim reasonably likely to be true. The background evidence does not tend to support the Appellant's claim. It suggests that active members of the OLF [Oromo Liberation Front] are treated very harshly indeed... Whilst the Appellant claims to have been beaten and raped, the background evidence suggests that she would have been severely tortured during interrogation. (ibid. 33)

The same study demonstrates that failure to be killed also indicated a lack of credibility. 'But they did not kill you', said an immigration officer to an applicant:

> It has been considered that you are not of interest to the authorities as they have had the opportunity to arrest, detain and kill you in the past but have not done so. (ibid. 33)

If they had killed the applicant, he would deserve asylum, but then he obviously could not come all the way to Europe to seek asylum. In other words, 'A good asylum seeker is a dead asylum seeker'.

In some cases, only death is assumed sufficient to testify to the authenticity of the claimed fear. In mid-February 2009, a 45-year-old Afghan man was taken to the emergency ward of a hospital in Stockholm. It was around midnight. The person who took him to the hospital disappeared as soon as nurses showed up. Ingesting a large number of pills, the man had wished to put an end to his life. He was saved after 20 hours in a respirator. The man, together with his family, wife and three daughters, had sought asylum in Sweden in 2005. The Migration Board rejected their application twice and a deportation order was issued. I asked the man why he had attempted suicide? He said he thought that his death would help his children have a chance to stay. He assumed that the Swedish authorities would then believe that their fear of returning was genuine and well-founded. When all the documents he had offered the authorities were deemed not 'enough' to prove, in the eyes of authorities, his and his family's suffering, he thought to attest to the authenticity of their case with his death. Not even his suicide attempt helped them. Another informant, Pari, a 60-year-old Iranian women, a failed asylum seeker who has lived clandestinely in Sweden for more than ten years, also sees her only chance to gain asylum in relation to her death. She used to say that her asylum would be granted on the day her death certificate is issued. Only her deceased body, her corpse, would have a chance of being believed.

Failed asylum seekers face a choice between complying with the deportation order, going back where they fled persecution, and migrant illegality. Migrant illegality is a consequence of the borders, not a cause of them.

In an American context, where irregular migration supplies considerable migrant labour, 'illegalization' is seen as a productive way of creating and maintaining a disciplined, servile and cheap reserve workforce (De Genova 2002:440). In Sweden, where irregular migration is linked to the asylum system, 'illegalization' is not merely a matter of market economics but also of national identity.

## Technologies of anti-citizenship

Seen through Foucaultian eyes, the 'production of criminality' is a way to create 'the norm'. 'Illegalization' of undocumented immigrants recreates and maintains a unified conception of the national identity of citizens (Behdad 1998). 'Migrant illegality' is configured in relation to what is considered *Swedishness*. Similarly, the ascribed 'primitive masculinity' of Muslim men is needed in constructing the 'civilized' Swedish masculinity (Khosravi 2009b).

Criminalizing undesirable non-citizens is pre-eminently a way to constitute citizenship (Isin 2002; Macklin 2007). Unidentified and therefore unmanageable masses of foreigners are contrasted to the ideal citizen. Technologies of citizenship aim to construct responsible, self-regulating, prudent, rational and ethical subjects. 'Failed' citizens are those who are 'unable or unwilling to enterprise their lives or manage their own risk, incapable of exercising responsible self-government, attached either to no moral community or to a community of anti-morality' (Rose 1999). The technologies of citizenship constitute a moralizing and 'responsibilizing' project, which aims to turn citizens into responsible and ethical subjects as opposed to irresponsible and unethical ones. In contrast to the ideal citizen, there is the anti-citizen, an individual who exists outside the ordinary regulatory system, one who violates established norms and who may constitute a risk to the safety and quality of life of 'normal' citizens.

Undocumented immigrants are seen as anti-citizens because they are considered burdens on society. They are thought to have a negative effect on welfare and the economy (their only costs to society are, ironically, the costs associated with their deportation). Above all, they are portrayed as a 'labour market problem'. They *take* jobs with low wages, which *weakens* collective agreements. In the end, they *endanger* the very existence of the welfare system (see Khosravi 2010). An anti-citizen is portrayed as a criminal, as lacking identity and as being irrational, irresponsible and immoral. An anti-citizen is someone who constitutes a risk to the wellbeing, virtue, values and norms of society (Inda 2006:177). As anti-citizens, undocumented immigrants are presumed to violate the 'ethical values' and 'morals' of citizens. Throughout my fieldwork, I have repeatedly encountered the image of undocumented immigrants as 'immoral', 'deceitful' and 'irresponsible' (Khosravi 2006).

## Anti-citizen I

*It is the autumn of 2005. Around 400 children with Pervasive Refusal Syndrome (PRS) have been registered nationally. They are the children of asylum-seeking families, most of which are from the former Soviet states. Since early 2005, there has been intensive debate in Sweden about this illness, its causes and whether it is found only in Sweden. The government-appointed experts have consistently claimed that the children were dissimulating and that it was all 'a gambit' to increase their families' chances of being allowed to stay in Sweden. The coordinator of the government inquiry has expressed her conviction that 'pervasive refusal syndrome among the children was caused by their parents who have forced them to lie' (Göteborgs-Posten, 27 April 2005). During the autumn of 2005, a raft of accusations was levelled against the families of children* who suffered from PRS in Sweden. In November, the Migration Board reported 13 parents of children with PRS to the police for having abused their children in order to present them as sick (Dagens Nyheter, 23 November 2005). Consequently, Minister for Public Health Morgan Johansson thought that these families ought not be given leave to remain (Dagens Nyheter, 28 November 2005). The media treated the families mercilessly. 'An anonymous businessman tells of Russian travel agencies instructing refugees on how to medicate their children into PRS' (Dagens Nyheter, 28 November 2005). 'Children with PRS have been sold and sexually abused' (Expressen, 1 December 2005). Parents of a child with PRS are 'suspected of having poisoned their daughter' (Dagens Nyheter, 19 January 2006).

Families of children with PRS are rendered suspect and demonized in these statements. In the form of repeated reports ordered by government and the Migration Board, these families went from being hapless victims needing protection to ruthless parents capable of torturing their children. They are presented as anti-citizens trespassing the ethical norms of the nation and constituting a *danger* to general family morality in Sweden.

## Anti-citizen II

During an interview with a section head at the Migration Board's detention centre north of Stockholm in November 2004, I asked about Simin, a middle-aged Kurdish woman who was then held at a police pre-trial detention centre awaiting deportation. Simin's husband was murdered by the police in front of his home in the Iranian part of Kurdistan. Her eldest son is in prison in Tehran. The other son lives 'illegally' in Athens. Simin, together with her youngest son, applied for asylum in Sweden in 2001. Their application was rejected and they went into hiding in June 2004. She was arrested by the police in October of that year and ended up in the Migration Board's detention centre. Desperate, she attempted suicide, which led to her being moved to the police pre-trial detention centre. When I asked the section head about Simin's suicide attempt, he became upset. He felt that the term 'suicide' did not appropriately describe Simin's actions: 'It was merely an attempt to harm herself to get attention'. The section head considered that there was a big difference between suicide attempts and 'attempts [by 'illegal' immigrants] to harm themselves'. 'To use the term "suicide" in this context was', according to him, 'unfair to all the young people in Sweden who are truly desperate and do commit suicide'.

Simin's action is set in opposition to the wellbeing of the nation ('young people in Sweden'). She is presented as an anti-citizen, whose suicide attempt is an affront to citizens.

## Anti-citizen III

*In June 2005, Bahman asked me to accompany him to a legal practice in central Stockholm. Bahman was a 'Dublin case'. In 2000, he had applied for asylum in a different EU Member State and been rejected. Helped by a human smuggler, he came to Sweden in 2001. Due to the Dublin Regulation, he has not dared apply for asylum in Sweden. I acted as an interpreter between Bahman and the lawyer. He told his story and asked what he could do. The lawyer was a middle-aged woman who was in the middle of packing when we entered. Her long-awaited holiday was going to begin after lunch. She was of the opinion that staying four years in Sweden without having applied for asylum would not help him with the Migration Board. Bahman asked whether he could tell the Migration Board that he had arrived in Sweden the same day as he applied for asylum. The lawyer became upset and said, 'In this country we are Protestants, and we do not lie'.*

As in Simin's case, here the dichotomization between 'honest' citizens and dishonest anti-citizens is clear. Bahman is set in contrast to the ethical (Protestant) values that, according to the lawyer, apply to the Swedish people.

The discursive construction of 'illegal immigrants' in the form of anti-citizens creates moral panic in society. Moral panic occurs when 'experts', mass media and authorities define and proclaim a 'danger to society' using statistics, diagnoses and prognoses.

The ethnographical examples above illustrate the conception of anti-citizens as penetrating the 'purity' of the welfare state, as constituting a 'danger'. With a view to protecting the welfare, social wellbeing and ethical values and norms of society, such individuals are placed under surveillance, locked up and deported. In this context, the deportation of every undocumented immigrant (anti-citizen) is seen by the officers at the Migration Board as a victory worth celebrating with champagne (see Khosravi 2009a).

To regulate, control and define what constitutes the undesirable group of undocumented immigrants, they are subject to removal policy while their reproduction is denied and controlled. The fertility of undocumented women is usually seen as posing a risk to the nation. Pregnancy is always a matter of concern for gatekeepers at borders. Pregnant women from poor countries are denied entry to the USA, since their children would automatically gain American citizenship if born inside the country. The female border transgressor, in her violation of the masculine militarized border regime, is seen as a double threat, as both a woman and an enemy.

In the case of undocumented migrants in Western countries, exclusion from the healthcare system especially affects undocumented female migrants (Khosravi 2010): in case of pregnancy, the lack of a right to antenatal care can have serious consequences for both mother and child. The lack of a right to prenatal care results in suffering and birth complications. For instance, in the case of HIV-infected and pregnant undocumented women, exclusion from the Swedish healthcare system means that the risk of infecting the child after birth increases almost 15 times (Ascher et al. 2008). Denying undocumented migrants healthcare is an attempt 'to govern the reproduction of an undesirable population' (Inda 2007:152). Undocumented women are encouraged not to become pregnant. Many of my female informants told me how they were 'advised' by various actors, from Migration Board officers to lawyers and even NGO activists, not to get pregnant. Asylum seekers were encouraged not to have children during the asylum application process. In a conference in the fall of 2006 in the small town of Gävle, north of Stockholm, an officer from the Migration Board said: 'As an asylum seeker, one should not marry. One should not fall in love. And it becomes awkward if one is going to have a baby with another asylum seeker. It is about control over one's sexuality' (*Artikel*, 14 March 2006, p. 3). In this context, love, sexuality and reproduction are no longer private/biological issues, but rather belong to the public and political spheres. Women's bodies become a battlefield where war is waged against immigrants. Luibhéid writes that undocumented women's bodies are 'sites where sexual, gender, racial, proletarianization and immigration processes all converge' (2002:132). The battle against undesirable migrants takes place on the terrain of migrant women's bodies (Inda 2007:153).

Denying these women care also sends a clear signal discouraging pregnancy. The desire of the authorities to control reproduction among undocumented migrants is manifested in allowing access to abortion but not to treatment of cancerous tumours (*Dagens Nyheter*, 11 May 2008).

The body of a pregnant undocumented immigrant no longer belongs to her but is a matter of national concern. Reproduction is no longer a natural act, a private biological choice, but a political issue. The dystopian film, *Children of Men*, tells the story of a world suffering from an unexplained infertility pandemic in 2027. Kee, a clandestine immigrant, is pregnant. Her pregnancy, her body, her unborn child – the focus of the film – is the concern of the authorities, who wish to find it, govern it and use it.

# 7
# The Right to Have Rights

*Right is what is good for the German people*

Adolf Hitler

Although the rights to healthcare, education for children, work and security – even for undocumented immigrants – are mentioned in various international and European conventions (Weissbrodt 2008; see also PICUM 2007), they are inaccessible to many of those who need them (cf. Romero-Ortuno 2004). This dilemma exemplifies the 'abstractedness' of the law, that is, its availability in terms of international conventions and declarations, and at the same time its inaccessibility to those concretely in need of it.

In other words, the 'Rights of Man' are for those people who do not have access to them. Hannah Arendt was the first to highlight the dilemma embedded in the condition of statelessness in the modern world, in an observation that still applies. She observed that the condition of statelessness not only rendered individuals immobile, but also caused them to be neglected and abandoned by the very conventions and declarations created for them. In 1949, one year after the UN Universal Declaration of Human Rights (UDHR) was proclaimed by the General Assembly of the United Nations, Arendt criticized the Declaration for both its lack of realism in ignoring problems of implementation and for its conceptual confusion.

Her paper was entitled 'The Rights of Man: What are they?' (this paper later formed part of her seminal book *The Origins of Totalitarianism*, 1951). For Arendt there was only *one* human right, and it was the 'right to have rights', or in other words, the right to claim one's rights. According to Arendt, the fundamental problem with the UDHR is that it is dependent on the nation-state system. Since human rights are based on civil rights, that is, citizens' rights, human rights can only be achieved through the nation-state system.

This means that human rights, as defined by the UDHR, can be materialized only in a political community. Loss of citizenship also means loss of human rights. The territorialization of human rights in the form of a system of nation-states reduces *human* rights to *citizen* rights. The nation-state system is the most globalized form of human organization. There is no place, no group on earth that is not affected by this system. According to this 'national order of things' (Malkki 1995b), all human beings are supposed to belong to a nation, real or imagined. Outside the nation-state system, there is no space for humanity. There is no space for something like the pure human being in herself, beyond legal and political status. Statelessness is regarded as a temporary status, even though it may last for generations, as in the case of the Palestinians. A stateless person is supposed to be (re)naturalized in the long term. A permanent status of statelessness, of being just a human being, is incompatible with the logic of the 'national order of things'. Those outside this order, the stateless, constitute excess population – read 'unnatural'. Only in this universal form of the organization of humanity (in terms of citizenship) 'could the loss of home and political status become identical with being expelled from humanity altogether' (Arendt 1994 [1951]:297), rendering one stateless, placeless and functionless (Bauman 2004:76). Such a stateless being is 'human waste' and disposable.

Perhaps it is for that reason that loss of citizenship is called *'denaturalization'* – becoming unnatural. Citizenship has become the *nature* of being human. Being outside the realm of citizenship means being outside nature. In the condition of statelessness, in the absence of citizenship, one becomes dehumanized (unnatural) and can be exposed to necropolitics – violence and death. Throughout the twentieth century, many nations and groups have been subjected to this dehumanization politics.

Starting with World War I, many European states began to introduce laws that permitted their own citizens to be denaturalized and denationalized: the first was France, in 1915, with regard to naturalized citizens of 'enemy' origins; in 1922, this example was followed by Belgium, which revoked the naturalization of citizens who had committed 'anti-national' acts during the war; in 1926, the Fascist regime in Italy passed a similar law concerning citizens who had shown themselves to be 'unworthy of Italian citizenship'; in 1933, it was Austria's turn, and so forth, until in 1935, the Nuremberg Laws divided German citizens into full citizens and citizens without political rights (Agamben 2000:17). We should not forget that the Nazis sent the German Jews to the concentration camps only after they were first robbed of their citizenship, and were thus rendered 'unnatural'.

The confusion, Arendt emphasized, engendered by the UDHR is illustrated when states deal with border transgressors. In the view of Hannah Arendt, there is only one human right and it is the right to membership in a political community. Only after gaining such membership does the individual have the right to claim her/his rights. Arendt correctly stated that the concept of human rights 'breaks down at the very moment when those who believed in it were confronted with people who had lost all other qualities except that they were still human' (Arendt 1994 [1951]:299) – namely, refugees and stateless people.

Concern for the 'universal' human rights of stateless people is virtually incompatible with states' concern for territorial sovereignty. This dilemma clarifies the paradox inherent in the 1948 UN Universal Declaration of Human Rights, which acknowledges the right to *emigrate* (Article 13) but not the right to *immigrate* (see Benhabib 2004:11). Article 15 emphasizes the right of all individuals 'to a nationality', but is silent on the obligation of states to grant immigrants such nationality. In other words, citizenship – the right to enjoy rights – is not a right in itself. Until that is the case, there will be two kinds of individual: human beings and *the rest*, or in Arendt's words, pariahs.

Outside this form of organized humanity, outside the realm of citizenship, there is no such place as a refuge. As a Jewish refugee from Nazi Germany who was placed in Camp Gurs in southwestern France, Arendt wrote 'We Refugees' (1943), a very short but perhaps the most impressive and illuminating text on the predicament of being *the rest*. She was impressively prophetic in her observation that:

[T]he outlawing of the Jewish people in Europe has been followed closely by the outlawing of most European nations. Refugees driven from country to country represent the vanguard of their people. (Arendt 1943:77)

Her observation is sadly still relevant to a huge number of stateless people sent back and forth between states. The destiny of the stateless Jews in the first half of the twentieth century has been, and still is being, repeated time and again in the case of other peoples around the world, denaturalized (rendered unnatural) and exposed to necropolitics. Hannah Arendt was not alive to witness how the destiny of the Jews of the *St. Louis* in 1939 was repeated by the Chinese migrants aboard the *Golden Venture* in 1993 and by 353 Iraqi asylum seekers aboard the *SIEV-X* in 2001 outside Australia. The passengers of the *St. Louis* are the 'defeated ancestors' of the passengers of the *SIEV-X*. More than 900 Jews fleeing the Third Reich boarded the *St. Louis* in 1939 in hope of finding refuge on the other side of the Atlantic. Banished by several countries, including the USA, the ship eventually re-crossed the Atlantic, returning to Europe to send several hundreds of its passengers to the death chambers. More than 60 years later, in October 2001, an estimated 421 mainly Iraqi asylum seekers departed Bandar Lampung in Indonesia on a small wooden fishing boat, heading towards Australia. According to survivor testimony, many were forced aboard at gunpoint by Indonesian police who supervised the loading. The overcrowded boat sank on 19 October inside the Australian aerial border protection surveillance zone. Approximately 146 children, 142 women and 65 men went down with the boat (Perera 2006; see also www.sievx.com, accessed June 2009).

Sixty years after Arendt, another displaced Jewish philosopher, Zygmunt Bauman, wonders 'to what extent the refugees' camps are laboratories where...the new liquid modern "permanently transient" pattern of life is put to the test and rehearsed. To what extent are the refugees' *nowhereville* the advanced samples of the world to come, and their inmates cast/pushed/forced into the role of its pioneer explorer?' (Bauman 2003:147).

The continuum of the predicament of statelessness, though striking different groups throughout modern history, is, in Walter Benjamin's words, 'the tradition of the oppressed' telling us that 'the state of emergency in which we live is not the exception but the rule'

(1999 [1940]:248). Refugees who have lost all rights but who no longer want to be assimilated at all costs to a new national identity, wanting instead to lucidly contemplate their condition, receive in exchange for assured unpopularity a priceless advantage: 'History is no longer a closed book to them and politics is no longer the privilege of Gentiles' (Arendt 1943:77).

Walter Benjamin, himself a stateless Jew escaping Nazi Germany, offers a different image of history. Rejecting the 'illusion of progress', in technological and economic terms, as the myth of modernity, Benjamin states that history is written in the interest of those who won in the past and are powerful in the present – hence its characterization as 'progress'. For the defeated, however, such 'progress' has meant catastrophes, the Holocaust, refugee camps, forced displacement, statelessness and slavery.

Looking at history from the standpoint of the defeated, Benjamin declared that remembering the *catastrophes*, defeats and victims of the past is necessary in order to struggle against oppression. *Zakhor* – remembering – is central to the ritual of the Jewish Passover, when Jews are called to remember their defeated ancestors, slaves in Egypt (Yerushalmi 2005). Only by remembering their defeated ancestors would there be a chance for the pariahs, the stateless people, to find a future.

## Hospitality

To write about borders is to talk about dichotomies: assimilating/ejecting, acceptance/rejection, and reception/expulsion. It is about hospitality (Dikeç 2002:229) and at the same time about hostility.

Hospitality is a central theme permeating this book. I would never have survived if it were not for the unconditional hospitality of strangers I met en route: people along the borders of Iran, Afghanstan, Pakistan and India, the Iranian woman and Afghan prostitute in New Delhi, and finally Swedish hospitality – albeit conditional. Hospitality begins at the very first moment of meeting 'the other', on the threshold, when and where the stranger – a refugee or migrant – asks for hospitality, in a language that is not their own. 'The foreigner is first of all foreign to the legal language in which the duty of hospitality is formulated, the right to asylum, its limits, its norms, policing, etc.' (Derrida 2000b:15).

This is the first act of hostility (Diken and Laustsen 2005:185) or, rather, the first act that renders hospitality conditional. The dialectic of welcoming and exclusion demonstrates that hospitality is regulated along the borders. Hospitality is modified in the nation-state system by intra-state agreement. It is conditional. Hospitality requires that the host be at home, that the host own the space to be opened to the guest; and this also means that the host can *close off* the space: 'Sovereignty is exactly the ability to close the door' (Diken and Laustsen 2005:185).

Conditional hospitality opens the gate only to those who 'deserve' it, those who have passports, valid visas, adequate bank statements, or invitations. Sovereignty regulates its borders to avoid 'unproductive' hospitality, to keep those out who cost, that is, refugees. Conditional hospitality, based on deservingness, targets 'good' 'productive' immigrants, skilled and assimilable, or a tiny number of 'powerless', 'voiceless' asylum seekers. The politics of conditional hospitality is also a nation-building process. In this manner, welcoming the 'deserving' 'genuine' refugees and expelling 'undeserving' 'bogus' ones is a sovereign act to reconfirm borders. The politics of hospitality is a politics of capacity and of the power of the host over the guest (Dikeç 2002:237). At the same time, it is the guest who confers meaning on the host: without hospitality, without the ability to offer hospitality, there is no master in the home (Rosello 2001).

'To dare to say welcome is perhaps to insinuate that one is at home here, that one knows what it means to be at home, and that at home one receives, invites, or offers hospitality, thus appropriating for oneself a place to *welcome* [*accueillir*] the other, or, worse, *welcoming* the other to appropriate for oneself a place and then speak the language of hospitality' (Derrida 1999:15–16).

Hospitality is not a matter of objective knowledge, but of lived experience (Derrida 2000a: 7). It is about recognizing 'the other' and giving space to the stranger. Hospitality, says Kant, 'is not a question of philanthropy but of right' (1957 [1795]:20). Following Kant, Benhabib believes that 'hospitality is not to be understood as a virtue of sociability, as the kindness and generosity one may show to strangers...hospitality is a right which belongs to all human beings' (Benhabib 2004:26).

Strangers have the right to hospitality 'by virtue of their common possession of the surface of the earth' (Kant 1957 [1795]:21). This 'natural' right to hospitality is a 'cosmopolitical' right, a right to protection and safety (Kant 1957 [1795]:20; see also Derrida 2008). Based on the right to nature (the surface of the earth), Kant depicts hospitality as a 'natural' law. However, as Benhabib correctly points out, the dilemma of the 'right' of hospitality is that it is situated at the boundaries of the polity, between norms of morality and positive law, between human rights and civil rights, between legally binding obligations and voluntary commitments (2006:22).

The concept of hospitality is problematic and ambivalent, and Derrida has underscored this ambivalence in a series of writings. The etymology of 'hospitality' indicates that the words *hospis* (host) and *hostes* (enemy) have common roots in Latin. For Derrida, hospitality is interlaced with hostility (Derrida 2000b:45); to reveal the ambivalence of the notion, he uses the term 'hostipitality' (2000a). The ambivalence of hospitality lies in the initial 'acceptance' of individuals through hospitality, but then keeping them strangers for generations, rejecting them because they are not like us and placing them in refugee camps, detention centres, or ghettos. What stateless, asylum seekers, undocumented migrants face today is a hostile hospitality.

As I'm writing these words in late September 2009, the French police are demolishing the refugee camp known as 'the Jungle', outside Calais in the north of France. The shantytown in the wood had been home to undocumented migrants, mostly from Iraq and Afghanstan, waiting for a chance to stow away under a truck or behind boxes of tomatoes in lorries to get themselves across la Manche – the English Channel – to England. At the time of the raid, 278 migrants, nearly half of them minors, were living in the camp (*The Guardian*, 22 September 2009). The dwellings made of scrap materials were bulldozed. The migrants have been detained and will be deported. In less than a few days a community, though not recognized by any authority and not appearing on any map, has been obliterated. After a few years of grudging 'tolerance' – conditional hospitality – it is time for hostility. The tolerance of strangers discloses the limit of a nation's hospitality. As Derrida says, tolerance is the opposite of hospitality and worse tolerance or lack of tolerance is a way to retain power and maintain control over the 'home' (Borradori 2003:127).

Decades ago, well-known anthropologist Claude Lévi-Strauss in his classic *Tristes Tropiques* made an interesting comparison between

how 'primitive' and modern societies deal with strangers and deviants. While the former were *anthropophagic* societies, the latter were
*anthropoemic* ones. *Anthropophagic* refers literally to 'eating the strangers up', thereby metaphorically eliminating the strangers' otherness
(see also Rosello 2001:30–31 for a discussion on cannibalism as a
radical form of hospitality). By swallowing strangers up, the non-
modern societies made them their own.

Modern societies, in contrast, are *anthropoemic* – they 'vomit' out
the strangers, and eject the undesirable individuals. '[T]hose which
practise cannibalism – that is, which regard the absorption of certain
individuals possessing dangerous powers as the only means of neu-
tralizing those powers and even of turning them to advantage – and
those which, like our own society, adopt what might be called the
practice of *anthropoemy* (from the Greek *émein*, to vomit); faced with
the same problem, the latter type of society has chosen the opposite
solution which consists in ejecting dangerous individuals from the
social body' (Lévi-Strauss (1997 [1955]:473).

The current 'hostipitality' targeting undocumented migrants is a
modernized version of the two strategies used for violently assimi-
lating immigrants or banishing them. While the practice of *anthropoemy*, 'vomiting' out strangers, occurs overtly and has become a
daily scene in today's world, the *anthropophagic* strategy is more
hidden and intrinsic in the nation-state system aiming to preserve
cultural homogeneity. This strategy refers to the 'nullification of a
stranger's ontological otherness by consuming his or her difference' (Marciniak 2006:17). An example of *anthropophagy* is the
forced name changing of new arrivals by Ellis Island officials, so
that the strangers' names would be 'pronounceable' by others in
the USA (ibid.). Almost a century later, immigrants, mainly from
the Middle East, still 'voluntarily' alter their names to have a
greater chance of attaining a better place in society (Arai and
Thoursie 2009).

The same week the Calais 'Jungle' was demolished (or, in Lévi-
Strauss's words, 'vomited' out by France), I saw *Welcome*, a compel-
ling and poignant film about undocumented migrants in the Calais
camp. The protagonist is a young Kurdish man who, after failing to
reunite with his beloved in other ways, aims to swim to England to
rejoin her. The film tacitly focuses on the ethics of hospitality, pre-
senting a Europe in which hospitality is criminalized. The swimming

instructor who helps and shelters the young Kurdish man is punished by the law for his acts of hospitality.

As a part of the struggle against irregular migration, hospitality itself has become a crime. The trend towards criminalizing assistance to undocumented migrants has intensified in Europe since the turn of the millennium (see PICUM 2002). Derrida deplores the 'crime of hospitality' and wonders '[w]hat becomes of a country, one must wonder, what becomes of a culture, what becomes of a language when it admits of a "crime of hospitality", when hospitality can become, in the eyes of the law and its representatives, a criminal offense?' (Derrida 2002:133).

Unconditional hospitality means being open to a person who is not like oneself, who is not the one wanted or expected. Hospitality is real only when it is extended to a person absolutely different from oneself. Unconditional hospitality entails recognizing the other's right to have rights – the basic right of human rights.

Borders and their necropolitics of wasted human lives make hospitality a pivotal issue in political ethics. As a question of openness and welcoming, 'ethic is so thoroughly coextensive with the experience of hospitality' (Derrida 2008:17). 'Hospitality is culture itself and not simply one ethic amongst others. Insofar as it has to do with the *ethos*, that is, the residence, one's home, the familiar place of dwelling, inasmuch as it is a manner of being there, the manner in which we relate to ourselves and to others, to others as our own or as foreigners, *ethics is hospitality*' (Derrida 2008:17, emphasis in the original).

Only in a world where the space of nation-states has been deconstructed and where citizens can recognize and accept non-citizens, refugees, the stateless and undocumented, only then is the political and ethical survival of humankind thinkable (see Agamben 2000:25).

'Democracies should be judged not only by how they treat their members but by how they treat their strangers' (Benhabib 1998:108). As Arendt puts it, openness to others is a precondition for humanity in every sense of the word (1983 [1955]: 24–25). Hospitality is not an option, but an urgent necessity if human beings want to have a future together.

# Coda

The last steps of this journey will be taken in the footsteps of Walter Benjamin across the France–Spain border. On 25 September 1940, Benjamin, a German Jew and one of the greatest thinkers of the twentieth century, with a handful of other stateless Jews, attempted to escape France into Spain.

After climbing all night across the Pyrenees, following a smugglers' route, the group reached Portbou, a border town on the Spanish side. Like other German Jews, Benjamin had been denaturalized (rendered unnatural and hence a *homo sacer*) by the Third Reich in 1939. His brother had already been deported to a labour camp. Throughout the 1930s, Benjamin's life was fragmented and nomadic: he moved from town to town and country to country in search of a safe place to live. He lived on support from his friends and with some help from universities in the USA. The only real home he had ever had since leaving Berlin was the Bibliothèque nationale in Paris, where he worked on his masterpiece, the *Arcades Project*. Unlike many other German Jews who had emigrated to Israel or the USA, he insisted on staying in Europe. He was not Jewish enough to live in Israel, not Marxist enough to be tolerated in Stalin's Moscow and not academic enough to get a job at an American university. His was a 'border persona' in all senses of the term. At the last minute, armed with a refugee passport, he headed to Lisbon to save his life. Europe had become 'uninhabitable'. However, the border had targeted him. He was denied entry to Spain because of the lack of a French exit visa. Fearing being handed over to the Gestapo, trapped between Vichy France and Franco's fascist Spain, Benjamin killed himself by ingesting morphine pills. The rest of the group, perhaps because of his tragic death, were allowed to cross the border into Spain the day after. However, the border selected Benjamin and forced him to be border.

Not even death could save him from violence of the border regime. Not even a dead Jewish body could be tolerated. He was buried as a Catholic, under the name 'Benjamin Walter' in a Catholic graveyard – despite his being a secularist who believed in materialist philosophy. His displacement endures even in death. The money left with him was only enough for five years' rent of the grave. In 1945, his remains were moved to a collective grave. Two memorial stones in the cemetery of Portbou bear his name, but his final burial place is unknown (see Leslie 2007). His death on the border reminds me of the death of Fatemeh-Kian, with whose suicide in a detention centre I started this book. One of the memorial stones in the cemetery bears a sentence from thesis VII of Benjamin's last manuscript, *Theses on the Concept of History* (1999 [1940]): 'There is no document of culture which is not at the same time a document of barbarism'. The monuments of nation-states are the monuments of borders, wars, genocides and racism. If the pyramids of Egypt bear witness to a ruthless slavery, and if colonial monuments are products of social and political oppression, war and bloodbath, today's gigantic construction projects in the form of the highest, most modern, buildings in Dubai testify to a more or less similar injustice and inequality imposed to immigrants (see Human Rights Watch 2006). Approaching history from the point of view of the defeated results in a philosophy of 'the organization of pessimism' – pessimism, not as a contemplative sentiment, but an active, organized, practical pessimism used as political strategy to prevent the imminent dangers looming over humanity (Löwy 2005:112). Benjamin's pessimism, organized in way similar to Kafka's, one of his 'defeated ancestors', forewarned that 'There is hope, but not for us', envisaging the catastrophes awaiting Europe.

This book is also organized along the lines of such pessimism, aiming to evoke memories of my defeated ancestors, stateless, slaves, Jews, Palestinians, Romani people, refugees, the undocumented and all those who have been forced to *be* the border.

*Zakhor!*

# Appendix: Destinations of my Co-Travellers

| | |
|---|---|
| Pour | Canada |
| Masoud | Canada |
| Latif | USA |
| Amir | The Netherlands |
| Mohammad | Germany |
| Hamid | Canada |
| Farshid | Sweden |
| Bahar | Canada |
| Alireza | Unknown |
| The siblings in room 304, Hotel Shalimar | Canada |
| Omid | Norway |
| Ali | Italy |
| Behrooz | Disappeared at the Pakistan–India border |
| Yousef | Iran |
| Omar | Unknown |
| Pooya | Canada |
| Hamed | USA |
| Ahmad | USA |
| Ramin | The Netherlands |
| Hoshang | The Netherlands |
| Siavash | The Netherlands |
| Kian senior | The Netherlands |
| Kian junior | UK/Sweden |
| Fariborz | Germany |
| Hamid | Germany |
| Hiva | India? |
| Hassan | Sweden |
| Hessam | Germany |
| Shahram 64 | Sweden |
| Henri | Unknown |
| Zaras | Committed suicide in Sweden |

| | |
|---|---|
| Reza gittarist | Sweden |
| Homayoun | Afghanstan |
| Nour | Russia/Afghanstan |
| Mahmood | Canada |
| Aziz | Jamaica |
| Said | Sweden |
| Babak, *Abre Sefid* (the White Cloud) | Committed suicide in Hotel Shalimar |

# Bibliography

Adey, Peter (2004) Secured and Sorted Mobilities: Examples from the Airport, *Surveillance & Society* 1(4): 500–519.

Adey, P. (2006) '"Divided We Move": The Dromologics of Airport Security and Surveillance,' in Monahan, T. (ed.) *Surveillance and Society: Technological Politics and Everyday Life*, New York: Routledge, 195–208.

Adorno, Theodor (2002 [1974]) *Minima Moralia*, New York: Verso.

*Afghanstan Opium Survey* (2007), Kabul: United Nations Office on Drugs and Crime.

Agamben, Giorgio (1995) We Refugees, *Symposium* 49(2): 114–119.

Agamben, Giorgio (1998) *Homo Sacer: Sovereign Power and Bare Life*, Stanford: Stanford University Press.

Agamben, Giorgio (2000) *Means without End: Notes on Politics*, Minneapolis: University of Minnesota Press.

Agier, Michel (2008) *On the Margins of the World: The Refugee Experience Today*, Cambridge: Polity Press.

Ali, Syed (2007) 'Go West Young Man': The *Culture* of *Migration* among Muslims in Hyderabad, India, *Journal of Ethnic and Migration Studies* 33(1): 37–58.

Amani, Mehdi (1992) *Les effets démographiques de la guerre Iran-Irak sur la population iranienne*, Paris: Institut national d'études démographiques.

Anderson, Benedict (1983) *Imagined Communities: Reflections on the Origin and Spread of Nationalism*, London: Verso.

van den Anker, Christien and Doomernik, Jeroen (2006) *Trafficking and Women's Rights*, Hampshire: Palgrave.

Anzaldúa, Gloria (1987) *Borderlands/La Frontera: The New Mestiza*, San Francisco: Spinsters/Aunt Lute.

Appadurai, Arjun (1996) *Modernity at Large*, Minneapolis: University of Minnesota Press.

Arai, Mahmood and Thoursie, Peter (2009) Renouncing Personal Names: An Empirical Examination of Surname Change and Earnings, *Journal of Labor Economics* 27(1): 127–147.

Arendt, Hannah (1943) We Refugees, *Menorah Journal* 31: 69–77.

Arendt, Hannah (1983 [1955]) *Men in Dark Times*, New York: Harvest Books.

Arendt, Hannah (1994 [1951]) *The Origins of Totalitarianism*, New York: Harvest Books.

Ascher, Henry, Björkman, Anders, Kjellström, Lars and Lindberg, Tor (2008) Diskriminering av papperslösa i vården leder till lidande och död Nytt lagförslag hot mot patienterna, vården och samhället, *Läkartidningen* 105(8): 538–541.

Augé, Mark (1995) *Non-places: Introduction to an Anthropology of Aupermodernity*, New York: Verso.

Balibar, Étienne (2002) *Politics and Its Other Scene*, New York: Verso.

Bauman, Zygmunt (1998) *Globalization: The Human Consequences*, Cambridge: Polity Press.

Bauman, Zygmunt (2003) *Liquid Love: On the Frailty of Human Bonds*, Cambridge: Polity Press.

Bauman, Zygmunt (2004) *Wasted Lives: Modernity and Its Outcasts*, Cambridge: Polity Press.

Beck, Ulrich (1992) *Risk Society: Towards a New Modernity*, London: Sage.

Behdad, Ali (1998) INS and Outs: Producing Delinquency at the Border, *Azlán* 23(1): 103–113.

Benhabib, Seyla (1998) On European Citizenship, *Dissent*, fall: 107–9.

Benhabib, Seyla (2004) *The Rights of Others: Aliens, Residents, and Citizens*, Cambridge: Cambridge University Press.

Benhabib, Seyla (2006) *Another Cosmopolitanism: Hospitality, Sovereignty, and Democratic Iterations*, (ed. Robert Post), Oxford: Oxford University Press.

Benjamin, Walter (1999 [1940]) *Illuminations*, London: Random House.

Benjamin, Walter (2007) *Walter Benjamin's Archive*, New York: Verso.

Bilger, Veronika, Hofmann, Martin and Jandl, Michael (2006) Human Smuggling as a Transnational Service Industry: Evidence from Austria, *International Migration* 44(4): 59–93.

Bohmer, Carol and Shuman, Amy (2008) *Rejecting Refugees: Political Asylum in the 21st Century*, London: Routledge.

Borradori, Giovanna (2003) *Philosophy in a Time of Terror: Dialogues with Jurgen Habermas and Jacques Derrida*, Chicago: University of Chicago Press.

Boyd, Monica (1989) Family and Personal Networks in International Migration: Recent Developments and New Agendas, *International Migration Review* 23(3): 638–670.

Buijs, Gina (1993) *Migrant Women: Crossing Boundaries and Changing Identities*, Oxford: Berg Publishers.

Butler, Judith (1993) Endangered/Endangering: Schematic Racism and White Paranoia, in Gooding-Williams, Robert (ed.) *Reading Rodney King/Reading Urban Uprising*, New York: Routledge, 15–22.

Cantú, Lionel (2002) De Ambiente: Queer Tourism and the Shifting Boundaries of Mexican Male Sexualities, *GLQ: A Journal of Lesbian and Gay Studies* 8(1–2): 139–166.

Cantú Lionel, Naples, Nancy A. and Vidal-Ortiz, Salvador (2009) *The Sexuality of Migration: Border Crossings and Mexican Immigrant Men*, New York: New York University Press.

Carling, Jørgen (2007) Migration Control and Migrant Fatalities at the Spanish-African Border, *International Migration Review* 41(2): 316–343.

Carpenter, Jan (2006) The Gender of Control, in Pickering, Sharon and Weber, Leanne (eds) *Borders, Mobility and Technologies of Control*, Dordrecht: Springer, 167–178.

Chelkowski, Peter and Dabashi, Hamid (1999) *Staging a Revolution: The Art of Persuasion in the Islamic Republic of Iran*, New York: New York University Press.

Chin, Ko-lin (1999) *Smuggled Chinese: Clandestine Immigration to the United States*, Philadelphia: Temple University Press.

Cohen, Jeffrey H. (2004) *The Culture of Migration in Southern Mexico*, Austin: University of Texas Press.

Cohen, Stanley (2002) *Folk Devils and Moral Panics*, London: Routledge.

Cornelius, Wayne (2001) Death at the Border: Efficacy and Unintended Consequences of US Immigration Control Policy, *Population and Development Review* 27(4): 661–685.

Cornelius, Wayne (2005) Controlling 'Unwanted' Immigration: Lessons from the United States, 1993–2004, *Journal of Ethnic and Migration Studies* 31(4): 775–794.

Coutin, Susan Bibler (2003) *Legalizing Moves: Salvadorian Immigrants' Struggle for U.S. Residency*, Ann Arbor: The University of Michigan Press.

Cresswell, Tim (2006) *On the Move: Mobility in the Modern Western World*, London: Routledge.

Dauvergne, Catherine (2008) *Making People Illegal: What Globalization Means for Migration and Law*, Cambridge: Cambridge University Press.

de Certeau, Michel (1984) *The Practice of Everyday Life*, Berkeley: University of California Press.

De Genova, N. (2002) 'Migrant Illegality and Deportability in Everyday Life', *Annual Review of Anthropology* 31: 419–447.

De Genova, Nicholas (2007) The Production of Culprits: From Deportability to Detainability in the Aftermath of 'Homeland Security', *Citizenship Studies* 11(5): 421–448.

Derrida, Jacques (1999) *Adieu: To Emmanuel Levinas*, Stanford: Stanford University Press.

Derrida, Jacques (2000a) Hostipitality, *Angelaki* 5(3): 3–17.

Derrida, Jacques (2000b) *Of Hospitality*, Stanford: Stanford University Press.

Derrida, Jacques (2002) *Negotiations: Interventions and Interviews, 1971–2001*, Stanford: Stanford University Press.

Derrida, Jacques (2008 [2001]) *On Cosmopolitanism and Forgiveness*, London: Routledge.

Dikeç, Mustafa (2002) Pera Peras Poros: Longing for Spaces of Hospitality, *Theory, Culture & Society* 19(1–2): 227–247.

Diken, Bulent and Laustsen, Carsten B. (2005) *The Culture of Exception: Sociology of Facing the Camp*, London: Routledge.

Donnan, Hastings and Wilson, Thomas M. (1999) *Borders: Frontiers of Identity, Nation and State*, Oxford: Berg.

Douglas, M. (1966) *Purity and Danger: An Analysis of Concepts of Pollution and Taboo*, London: Routledge & Kegan Paul.

Dow, Mark (2007) Designed to Punish: Immigrant Detention and Deportation, *Social Research* 74(2): 533–546.

Drakulić, Slavenska (1987) *How We Survived Communism and Even Laughed*, New York: Vintage.

Ellis, Carolyn and Bochner, Arthur P. (2000) Autoethnography, Personal Narrative, Reflexivity: Researcher as Subject, in Denzin, N. and Lincoln, Y. (eds) *The Handbook of Qualitative Research*, Thousand Oaks: Sage, 733–768.

Ellison, Ralph (1987 [1952]) *Invisible Man*, Harmondsworth: Penguin.

Espín, Oliva (1999) *Women Crossing Boundaries: The Psychology of Immigration and the Transformations of Sexuality*, London: Routledge.

Ewing, Katherine (2008) *Stolen Honor: Stigmatizing Muslim Men in Berlin*, Stanford: Stanford University Press.

Falcón, Sylvanna (2001) Rape as a Weapon of War: Advancing Human Rights for Women at the U.S.–Mexican Border, *Social Justice* 28(2): 31–50.

Falcón, Sylvanna (2007) Rape as Weapon of War: Militarized Rape at the U.S.-Mexican Border, in Segura, Denis and Zavella, Patricia (eds) *Women and Migration: In the U.S.-Mexican Borderlands*, Durham: Duke University Press, 203–223.

Fanon, Frantz (1994 [1952]) *Black Skin, White Masks*, New York: Grove Press.

Ferguson, James (1999) *Expectations of Modernity: Myths and Meanings of Urban Life on the Zambian Copperbelt*, Los Angeles: University of California Press.

Foucault, Michel (1977) *Discipline and Punish: The Birth of the Prison*, London: Allen Lane.

GAO-06-770 (2006) *Illegal Immigration: Border-Crossing Deaths Have Doubled Since 1995*, United States Government Accountability Office, August.

Garthwaite, Gene (2009) *Khans and Shahs: A History of the Bakhtiyari Tribe in Iran*, London: I.B. Tauris.

GCIM (2005) *Migration in an Interconnected World: New Directions for Action*, Geneva: Global Commission on International Migration.

Gebrewold, Belachew (2007) *Africa and Fortress Europe: Threats and Opportunities*, Hampshire: Ashgate.

Gellner, Ernest (1990) *Nation and Nationalism*, Ithaca: Cornell University Press.

Ghosh, Amitav (1986) The Imam and the Indian, *Granta* 20 (Winter): 135–146.

Gouverneur, Cedric (2002) Iran Loses its Drugs War, *Le Monde Diplomatique*, March.

Gurak, Douglas and Caces, Fe (1992) Migration Networks and the Shaping of Migration Systems, in Kritz, Mary, Lim, Lin and Zlotnick, Hania (eds) *International Migration System: A Global Approach*, Oxford: Claredon Press, 150–176.

Hagan, Jacqueline M. (2008) *Migration Miracle: Faith, Hope and Meaning*, Cambridge: Harvard University Press.

Hahn, Hans P. and Klute, Georg (2007) *Cultures of Migration: African Perspectives*, Münster: LIT Verlag.

Hannerz, Ulf (1997) Borders, *International Social Science Journal* 157: 537–548.

Hicks, Heather J. (2007) Suits vs. Skin: Immigration and Race in Men in Black, *Arizona Quarterly* 63(2): 109–134.

Holmes, Seth M. (2007) 'Oaxacans like to work bent over': The Naturalization of Social Suffering among Berry Farm Workers', *International Migration* 45(3): 39–68.

Horst, Cindy (2006) *Transnational Nomads: How Somalis Cope with Refugee Life in the Dadaab Camps of Kenya*, Oxford: Berghahn Books.

Human Rights Watch (1995) *Cross the Line: Human Rights Abuses Along the U.S. Border with Mexico Persist amid Climate of Impunity*, (New York: Human Rights Watch) 7(4).

Human Rights Watch (2006) *Building Towers, Cheating Workers*, New York: Human Rights Watch.

Hunt, Krista and Rygiel, Kim (2006) *(En)gendering the War on Terror: War Stories and Camouflaged Politics*, Hampshire: Ashgate.

Içduygu, Ahmet and Toktas, Sule (2002) How Do Smuggling and Trafficking Operate via Irregular Border Crossings in the Middle East? Evidence from Fieldwork in Turkey, *International Migration* 40(6): 25–54.

IDMC (2008) Afghanstan: Increasing Hardship and Limited Support for Growing Displaced Population, at www.internal-displacement.org (accessed 28 October 2008).

Inda, Jonathan X. (2006) *Targeting Immigrants: Government, Technology, and Ethics*, Oxford: Blackwell.

Inda, Jonathan X. (2007) The Value of Immigrant Life, in Segura, Denis and Zavella, Patricia (eds) *Women and Migration: In the U.S.-Mexican Borderlands*, Durham: Duke University Press, 134–157.

IOM (2008) *Trafficking in Persons in Afghanstan*, International Organization for Migration, June.

Isin, Engin F. (2002) *Being Political: Genealogies of Citizenship*, Minneapolis: University of Minnesota.

Jackson, Michael (2007) *Excursions*, Durham: Duke University Press.

Jazayery, Leila (2002) The Migration-Development Nexus: Afghanstan Case Study, *International Migration* 40(5): 232–254.

Joly, Danièle, Kelly, Lynette and Nettleton, Clive (1997) *Refugees in Europe: The Hostile New Agenda*, London: Minority Rights Group.

Kafka, Franz (1999 [1925]) *The Trial*, Berlin: Schocken.

Kafka, Franz (2003 [1914]) *Metamorphosis and Other Stories*, New York: Barnes & Noble.

Kandel, William and Massey, Douglas S. (2002) The Culture of Mexican Migration: A Theoretical and Empirical Analysis, *Social Forces* 80(3): 981–1004.

Kant, Immanuel (1957 [1795]) *Perpetual Peace*, New York: The Liberal Arts Press.

Khemiri, Jonas H. (2006) *Montecore: en unik tiger*, Stockholm: Norstedts.

Khosravi, Shahram (2006) Territorialiserad mänsklighet: irreguljära immigranter och det nakna livet, in Paulina de los Reyes (ed.) *Välfärdens gränser: ett villkorat medborgarskap i diskrimineringens skugga* (SOU), 283–310.

Khosravi, Shahram (2008) *Young and Defiant in Tehran*, Philadelphia: University of Pennsylvania Press.

Khosravi, Shahram (2009a) Detention and Deportation of Asylum Seekers in Sweden, *Race & Class* 50(4): 30–56.

Khosravi, Shahram (2009b) Gender and Ethnicity among Iranian Men in Sweden, *Journal of Iranian Studies* 42(4): 591–609.

Khosravi, Shahram (2010) An Ethnography of Migrant 'Illegality' in Sweden: Included yet Excluded, *Journal of International Political Theory* 6(1): 95–116.

Koser, Khalid (2008) Why Migrant Smuggling Pays, *International Migration* 46(2): 3–26.

Koser Akcapar, Sebnem (2006) Conversion as a Migration Strategy in a Transit Country: Iranian Shiites Becoming Christians in Turkey, *International Migration Review* 4: 817–853.

Kronenfeld, Daniel (2008) Afghan Refugees in Pakistan, *Journal of Refugee Studies* 21(1): 43–63.

Kumar, Amitava (2000) *Passport Photos*, Los Angeles: University of California Press.

Leslie, Esther (2007) *Walter Benjamin*, London: Reaktion Books.

van der Leun, Joanne (2003) *Looking for Loopholes: Processes of Incorporation of Illegal Immigrants in the Netherlands*, Amsterdam: Amsterdam University Press.

Lévi-Strauss, Claude (1997 [1955]) *Tristes Tropiques*, New York: Random House.

Liempt, van Ilse (2007) *Navigating Borders: Inside Perspectives on the Process of Human Smuggling into the Netherlands*, Amsterdam: Amsterdam University Press.

Löfgren, Orvar (1999) Crossing Borders: The Nationalization of Anxiety, *Ethnologia Scandinavica* 29: 5–27.

Löwy, Michael (2005) *Fire Alarm: Reading Walter Benjamin's 'On the Concept of History'*, New York: Verso.

Lubkemann, Stephen (2008) *Culture in Chaos: An Anthropology of the Social Condition in War*, Chicago: University of Chicago Press.

Luibhéid, Eithne (2002) *Entry Denied: Controlling Sexuality at the Border*, Minneapolis: University of Minnesota Press.

Luibhéid, Eithne (2004) Heteronormativity and Immigration Scholarship: A Call for Change, *GLQ: A Journal of Lesbian and Gay Studies* 10(2): 227–235.

Luibhéid, Eithne (2008) Sexuality, Migration, and the Shifting Line Between Legal and illegal Status, *GLQ: A Journal of Lesbian and Gay Studies* 14(2–3): 289–315.

Macklin, Audrey (2007) Who is the Citizen's Other? Considering the Heft of Citizenship, *Theoretical Inquiries in Law* 8: 475–508.

Mai, Nicola (2001) 'Italy is Beautiful': The Role of Italian Television in the Albanian Migratory Flow to Italy, in King, R. and Wood, N. (eds) *Media and Migration: Constructions of Mobility and Difference*, London: Routledge, 95–109.

Malkki, Liisa (1992) National Geographic: The Rooting of Peoples and the Territorialization of National Identity among Scholars and Refugees, *Cultural Anthropology* 7(1): 24–44.

Malkki, Liisa (1995a) *Purity and Exile: Violence, Memory, and National Cosmology among Hutu Refugees in Tanzania*, Chicago: University of Chicago Press.

Malkki, Liisa (1995b) Refugees and Exile: From 'Refugee Studies' to the National Order of Things, *Annual Review of Anthropology* 24: 495–523.

Malkki, Liisa (1997) Speechless Emissaries: Refugee, Humanitarianism, and Dehistoricization, in Olwig, Fog and Hastrup, Kristen (eds) *Siting Culture*, London: Routledge, 223–254.

Marciniak, Katarzyna (2006) *Alienhood: Citizenship, Exile, and the Logic of Difference*, Minneapolis: University of Minnesota Press.

140   *Bibliography*

Martin, Jeannett (2007) What's New with the Been-to? *Educational Migrants, Return from Europe and Migrant's Culture in Urban Southern Ghana,* in Hahn, Hans P. and Klute, Georg (eds) *Cultures of Migration: African Perspectives,* Münster LIT Verlag, 203–238.

Martínez, Elizabeth (1998) *De Colores Means All of Us: Latina Views for a Multi-Colored Century,* Cambridge, Mass.: South End Press.

Massey, Douglas (1986) The Social Organization of Mexican Migration to the United States, *Annals of AAPSS* 487: 102–113.

Mbembe, Achille (2003) Necropolitics, *Public Culture* 15(1): 11–40.

McMurray, David A. (2001) *In and Out of Morocco: Smuggling and Migration in a Frontier Boomtown,* Minneapolis: University of Minnesota Press.

Mehran, Sir Alfred and Donkin, Andrew (2004) *The Terminal Man,* London: Corgi Books.

Michalowski, Raymond (2007) Border Militarization and Migrant Suffering: A Case of Transnational Social Injury, *Social Justice* 34(2): 62–76.

Monsutti, Alessandro (2007) Migration as a Rite of Passage: Young Afghans Building Masculinity and Adulthood in Iran, *Iranian Studies* 40(2): 167–185.

Nafisi, Rasool (1992) Education and the Culture of Politics in the Islamic Republic of Iran, in Farsoun, Samih K. and Mashayekhi, Mehrdad (eds) *Iran: Political Culture in the Islamic Republic,* London: Routledge.

Noll, Gregor and Popovic, Aleksandra (2006) Flyktingstatus – en marginaliserad resurs I svensk asylrätt?, *Juridisk Tidskrift* 4: 834–865.

Papadopoulou-K, Aspasia (2008) *Transit Migration: The Missing Link between Emigration and Settlement,* London: Palgrave.

Perera, Suvendrini (2006) They Give Evidence: Bodies, Borders and the Disappeared, *Social Identities* 12(6): 637–656.

Petros, M. (2005) *The Cost of Human Smuggling and Trafficking,* Global Migration Perspectives, 31, Geneva: Global Commission on International Migration.

PICUM (2002) Penalizing and Criminalizing Assistance Provided to Undocumented Migrants, Brussels: Picum.

PICUM (2007) Undocumented Migrants Have Rights: An Overview of the International Human Rights Framework, Brussels: Picum.

Pratt, Anna (2005) *Securing Borders: Detention and Deportation in Canada,* Vancouver: The University of British Columbia Press.

Pratt, Mary Louise (1992) *Imperial Eyes: Travel Writing and Transculturation,* London: Routledge.

Raj, Kartik Varada (2006) Paradoxes on the Borders of Europe, *International Feminist Journal of Politics* 8(4): 512–534.

Rajaram, Prem Kumar and Grundy-Warr, Carl (2004) The Irregular Migrant as Homo Sacer: Migration and Detention in Australia, Malaysia, and Thailand, *International Migration* 42(1): 33–63.

Reed-Danahay, Deborah (1997) *Auto/Ethnography: Rewriting the Self and the Social,* Oxford: Berg.

Richmond, Anthony (1994) *Global Apartheid,* Oxford: Oxford University Press.

Romero-Ortuno, Roman (2004) Access to Health Care for Illegal Immigrants in the EU: Should we be Concerned?, *European Journal of Health Law* 11: 245–272.

Rose, Nikolas (1999) *Powers of Freedom: Reframing Political Thought*, New York: Cambridge University Press.

Rosello, Mireille (2001) *Postcolonial Hospitality: The Immigrant as Guest*, Stanford: Stanford University Press.

Rouse, R. (1991) Mexican Migration and Social Space of Postmodernism, *Diaspora* 1(1): 8–23.

Rumford, Chris (2006) Theorizing Borders, *European Journal of Social Theory* 9(2): 155–169.

Sadr, Shadi (1386/2007) Motalebe-ye Tabeiyat-e Madari, *Goft-o-Gu* 50: 61–82.

Said, Edward (2001 [1984]) Reflections on Exile, in Roberson, Susan (ed.) *Defining Travel: Diverse Visions*, Jackson: University Press of Mississippi, 178–189.

Saint, Tony (2005) *Refusal Shoes*, London: Serpent's Tail.

Salter, Mark B, (2004) Passports, Mobility, and Security: How Smart Can the Border Be?, *International Studies Perspectives* 5(1): 71–91.

Sartre, Jean-Paul (1956) *Being and Nothingness: An Essay on Phenomenological Ontology*, New York: Philosophical Library.

Sartre, Jean-Paul (1989 [1944]) *No Exit and Three Other Plays*, New York: Vintage.

Sayad, Abdelmalek (1999) *La double absence: Des illusions de l'emigre aux souffrances de l'immigre*, Paris: Seuil.

Schütz, Anton (2000) Thinking the law with and against Luhmann, Legendre and Agamben, *Law and Critique* 11(2): 107–136.

Sen, Amartya (1981) *Poverty and Famines: An Essay on Entitlement and Deprivation*, Oxford: Oxford University Press.

Shahrani, Nazif (1995) Afghanstan's Muhajirin: Politics of Mistrust and Distrust of Politics, in Valentine, D. and Knudsen, J. (eds) *Mistrusting Refugees*, Los Angeles: University of California Press.

Simon, Jonathan (1998) Refugees in a Carceral Age: The Rebirth of Immigration Prisons in the United States, *Public Culture* 10(3): 577–607.

Simon, Jonathan (2007) *Governing through Crime: How the War on Crime Transformed American Democracy and Created a Culture of Fear*, New York: Oxford University Press.

Stoller, Paul (2009) *The Power of the Between: An Anthropological Odyssey*, Chicago: University of Chicago Press.

Stychin, Carl F. (2000) 'A Stranger to Its Laws': Sovereign Bodies, Global Sexualities, and Transnational Citizens, *Journal of Law and Society* 27(4): 601–625.

Szörényi, Anna (2006) The Images Speak for Themselves? Reading Refugee Coffee-table Books, *Visual Studies* 21(1): 24–41.

Talpos, Ioan, Dima, Bogdan, Mutascu, Mihai and Enache, Cosmin (2008) *Culture and Migration: A Tale about Fear and Hope (with an Empirical Analysis on European Union Case)* Working paper, Munich 2008, at: http://mpra.ub.uni-muenchen.de/7746/ (accessed 11 January 2010).

Tamas, Gellert (2003) *Lasermannen*, Stockholm: Ordfront.

Tapper, Richard (1983) *The Conflict of Tribe and State in Iran and Afghanstan*, New York: St. Martin's Press.

Teo, Sin Y. (2003) Imagining Canada: The Cultural Logics of Migration Amongst PRC Immigrants, *Working Paper Series* No. 03–16. Vancouver: Vancouver Centre of Excellence.

Tirman, John (2004) *The Maze of Fear: Security and Migration after 9/11*, New York: The New Press.

Torpey, John (2000) *The Invention of the Passport: Surveillance, Citizenship and the State*, Cambridge: Cambridge University Press.

Treiber, Magnus (2007) Dreaming of a Good Life – Young Urban Refugees from Eritrea Between Refusal of Politics and Political Asylum, in Hahn, Hans P. and Klute, Georg (eds) *Cultures of Migration: African Perspectives*, Münster LIT Verlag.

Trueman, Trevor (2009) *Reasons for Refusal: An Audit of 200 Refusals of Ethiopian Asylum-seekers in England*, Conference paper presented at Seeking Refuge: Caught between bureaucracy, lawyers and public indifference?, School of Oriental and African Studies, London, 16–17 April.

Turner, Victor (1967) *The Forest of Symbols: Aspects of Ndembu Ritual*, Ithaca, Cornell University Press.

Turton, David (2003) *Conceptualising Forced Migration*, Working Papers, No. 12, Oxford: Refugee Studies Centre, Oxford University.

UNHCR (2009) *Briefing Notes*, 9 January, at www.unhcr.org.

Utas, Mats (2005) Victimcy, Girlfriending, Soldiering: Tactic Agency in a Young Woman's Social Navigation of the Liberian War Zone, *Anthropological Quarterly* 78(2): 403–430.

Wali, Sima (1990) *Female Refugee Victims of Sexual Violence: Rape Trauma and its Impact on Refugee Resettlement*, Manuscript, Washington: D.C. RefWID.

Warren, Kay B. (1997) Narrating Cultural Resurgence: Gender and Self-Representation for Pan-Mayan Writers, in Reed-Danahay, Deborah (ed.) *Auto/Ethnography: Rewriting the Self and the Social*, Oxford: Berg.

Weiner, Myron (1993) *International Migration and Security*, Boulder, CO: Westview Press.

Weissbrodt, David (2008) *Human Rights of Non-Citizens*, Oxford: Oxford University Press.

Welch, Michael (2002) *Detained: Immigration Laws and the Expanding I.N.S. Jail Complex*, Philadelphia, PA: Temple University Press.

Welch, Michael and Schuster, Liza (2005) Detention of Asylum Seekers in the UK and USA: Deciphering Noisy and Quiet Constructions, *Punishment & Society* 7(4): 397–417.

Willen, Sarah S. (2007) Toward a Critical Phenomenology of 'Illegality': State Power, Criminalization, and Abjectivity among Undocumented Migrant Workers in Tel Aviv, Israel, *International Migration* 45(3): 8–38.

Williams, Patricia J. (1991) *The Alchemy of Race and Rights*, Cambridge: Harvard University Press.

Wilson, Dean and Weber, Leanne (2008) Surveillance, Risk and Preemption on the Australian Border, *Surveillance & Society* 5(2): 124–141.

World Bank (2008) *Migration and Remittances*, Washington: The World Bank.
*World Refugee Survey* (2007), Arlington: USCRI.
Wright, Terence (2000) *Refugees on Screen*, Working Paper, No. 5. Oxford: Refugee Studies Centre, University of Oxford.
Yaghmaian, Behzad (2005) *Embracing the Infidel: Stories of Muslim Migrants on the Journey West*, New York: Delacorte Press.
Yerushalmi, Yosef Hayim (2005) *Zakhor: Jewish History and Jewish Memory*, Washington: University of Washington Press.

## Films

*Angst essen Seele auf (Ali: Fear Eats the Soul)*, by Rainer Werner Fassbinder, 1973.
*Baran*, by Majid Majidi, 2001.
*Bicycle Ran*, by Mohsen Makhmalbaf, 1998.
*Casablanca*, by Michael Curtiz, 1942.
*Children of Men*, by Alfonso Cuarón, 2006.
*Djomeh*, by Hassan Yektapanah, 2000.
*The Guests of Hotel Astoria*, by Reza Alamehzadeh, 1989.
*Heiran*, by Shalizeh Arefpoor, 2009.
*In this World*, by Michael Winterbottom, 2002.
*Lasermannen*, by Mikael Marcimain, Swedish Television, 2005.
*Men in Black*, by Barry Sonnenfeld, 1997.
*Midnight Express*, by Alan Parker, 1978.
*Mississippi Burning*, by Alan Parker, 1988.
*Tenant*, by Roman Polanski, 1976.
*The Terminal*, by Steven Spielberg, 2004.
*Ulysses's Gaze*, by Theo Angelopoulos, 1995.
*Welcome*, by Philippe Lioret, 2009.
*Well-Founded Fear*, by Shari Robertson and Michael Camerini, 2000.

## Other references

*Aftonbladet*, 7 November 1991.
*Asharq Al-Awsat*, 4 December 2008.
*Dagens Nyheter*, 23 November 2005.
*Dagens Nyheter*, 28 November 2005.
*Mehr News*, 22 January 1384/2005.
*Dagens Nyheter*, 19 January 2006.
*Dagens Nyheter*, 11 May 2008.
*Expressen*, 1 December 2005.

*Göteborgs-Posten*, 27 April 2005.
*Artikel*, 14 March 2006.
*Dagens Nyheter*, 27 November 2007.
*BBC Persian*, 3 May 2007.
*BBC Persian*, 18 October2008.
*The Irrawaddy*, 20 October 2008.
SR (Swedish Radio), 21 January 2008.
*Yemen Times*, 21 February 2007.
www.unitedagainstracism.org
www.amirheidari.com
www.sievx.com

# Index

polluted/polluting bodies, 3
poverty, 113
pregnancy, 119–20
prenatal care, 119–20
primitive masculinity, 77–8, 115
prison, 17–18, 20–1, 101–2
profiling, 66
public/private life, 81–3, 97
purity/impurity, 2–3

quasi-citizenship, 98, 99
Quetta, Pakistan, 30–1

race, 77
racism, 26, 83–4, 89, 95, 97, 98
rape, 40–1, 81, 114
reception/expulsion, 125
refugee camps
   in Sweden, 69–75
   treatment in, 70–1
refugee spies, 35–6
refugee status, 33
refugeeness, 71–4
refugees
   *see also* asylum seekers
   Afghan, 18–19
   clientization of, 71
   expectations about, 72–3
   'genuine', 31, 33–5
   images of, 73
   repatriation of, 92–3
   'risky', 111–15
   status of, 70–3
religion, 51–2
remembering, 125
reproduction, 119–20
rich-poor borders, 28
rights, 121–5
risk society, 112
robbery, by border guards, 19

sacrifice, 29
Saint, Tony, 63
Sartre, Jean-Paul, 76
Scandinavia, 58
sea routes, 102, 103

second-grade passports, 61
secrecy, 44
security-migration nexus, 100
separation, from family, 22–3
September 11, 2001, 77, 100
sex roles, 48
sexual abuse, 39, 40–1
sexuality, 119–20
shame, 24, 40, 66–7, 86–8, 94
*SIEV-X*, 124
Sir Alfred, 65
Sisyphus, 75
smuggling, *see* human smugglers/
   smuggling
smuggling routes, 102
social networks, 50–1
Somali migrants, 103
sovereignty, 2–3
Soviet Union, 25
*St. Louis*, 124
state, 113
state sovereignty, 2
statelessness, 121, 122, 123–5
strangers, 127–8
suffering
   of asylum seekers, 113–15
   as political issue, 113
suicide, 117–18
Sweden, 38, 54, 62, 66
   asylum regime in, 99–105
   deportation from, 99–100
   refugee camp in, 69–75
Swedish border, 98

technologies of citizenship, 115–16
*Tenant, The* (film), 76
territory, 2
terrorism, 77, 100
tolerance, 127
tolerant zones, 48
transformation, 86
transit halls, 65
transnationalism, 30
travel bans, 85–6
*Trial, The* (Kafka), 82
Turkey-Greece border, 53

CPSIA information can be obtained
at www.ICGtesting.com
Printed in the USA
LVOW03s2313110917
548301LV00010B/197/P

9 780230 336742